HEAVENLY ARMY OF ANGELS

Bob and Penny Lord

Journeys of Faith
1-800-633-2484

Cover Photo
The Translation of the Holy House of Loreto
by G. B. Tiepolo
Used with permission of the Congregazione Universale della
Santa Casa - Loreto, Italy

Dedication

For the last five years, we have concentrated our writing and talks on the subject of Power, the Power of Jesus in the Eucharist, the Power Jesus has given His Mother Mary, Powerful Men in the Church, Powerful Women in the Church, and now the Power of the Angels, God's Holy Messengers. Why has the Lord given us such an urgency to write on these subjects?

We are convinced there is a great necessity to impress upon the people of God that we are not hopeless; we are not helpless. On the contrary, we have been given an overwhelming amount of strength by Our Lord Jesus to sustain us on the journey, especially during the rough times, which we seem to be in all the time. We have a lot going for us. Jesus continues to keep His promise, "*I will be with you always, until the end of the world.*"

We would like to acknowledge and thank those strong men and women who know how important this book is, and have dedicated vast amounts of time and effort, against what seemed like insurmountable odds, sometimes in the face of ridicule by those who don't believe in Angels, to bring you and us these strong intercessors, our cousins, the Angels.

Pope John Paul II - A special gift from the Father, our Pope affirms all the beliefs in Angels we have held onto, which we espouse so firmly in this book. We thank him for his Catechetical teachings, which he gives every Wednesday at the General Audiences. It is in the context of these talks, that he elaborates on Angels, on personal Guardian Angels, as well as the whole Heavenly Army of Angels.

Mother Angelica and the Monastery of Our Lady of the Angels, Birmingham, Alabama - It was in this peaceful, yet powerful setting, this contradiction of a nun running a television network from a cloistered convent, where the Angels are given so much importance, that Our Lord Jesus inspired us to raise up the Angels to the level of consciousness of the people.

Padre Giuseppe Santarelli - Congregation of the Holy House - Loreto, Italy - In his great desire to make the name of the Holy House of Loreto known worldwide, Fr. Santarelli has been an enormous help, not only in doing the chapter on the Angels and the Holy House of Loreto, but he has helped us immeasurably in taping the Holy House for our television documentary, which has received outstanding reception, since its release in August, 1991, and its first showings on EWTN.

Padre Filippo de Michele - Cave of St. Michael, Gargano, Italy Fr. Filippo has been very instrumental over the years in giving us information on the history and spirituality of the Cave of St. Michael, which was not available through normal channels. In 1990, he allowed us to tape a documentary on the Cave of St. Michael, and he allows us to teach our pilgrims about the shrine, right at the altar of St. Michael.

Fr. Joseph Pio, and Fr. Alessio Parente - Our Lady of Grace Monastery, San Giovanni Rotondo, Italy - for their ongoing cooperation, and courtesy to us and to our pilgrims, each time we go there. They have made information on Padre Pio and the Angels so easy to obtain.

Our greatest debt of thanks goes to all the people who have such a devotion to the *Heavenly Army of Angels*. It is your enthusiasm and encouragement, which has given us the impetus to keep going when it became difficult. Your love of the Angels, and your confidence in the Lord working through us to bring you the compassion and power of the Angels, has made this book possible.

Jesus loves you - Mary loves you - the Angels love you
and we love you!

Table of Contents

Introduction   7
1. What and who are the Angels   16
2. The Angels bridge the Gap   29
3. The Guardian Angels   39
4. Lucifer's army of fallen angels   57
5. Jesus and the Angels   75
6. St. Michael's Cave and Mountain   89
7. Mary and the Angel Gabriel   111
8. Our Lady of Pilar and the Angels   119
9. The Angels and The Holy House   131
10. Mary and the Angels at Knock   151
11. Angels and the Miraculous Medal   155
12. Fatima and the Angel   169
13. Angels in Medjugorje?   180
14. Saints and the Angels   191
        St. Stephen   191
        St. Peter in Chains   193
        An Angel comes to St. Paul   195
        St. Augustine & The Holy Trinity   197
        St. Patrick and the Angels   199
        St. Francis and the Seraph Angel   204
        St. Clare of Assisi   208
        St. Thomas Aquinas   209
        St. Margaret of Cortona   211
        St. Catherine of Siena   215
        St. Joan of Arc   218
        St. Frances of Rome   225
        St. Teresa of Avila   229
        St. Don Bosco and il Grigio   234
        St. Gemma Galgani   236
15. The Popes and the Angels   247
Bibliography   255

The Hour of the Angelic Powers

given by our Lady to Fr. Gobbi September 29, 1990
"You are celebrating today the feast of the Archangels, Gabriel, Raphael and Michael, and you are invoking their protection. In these times of the great tribulation, I urge you to live in a union of life with the Angels of the Lord. Today they have an important task to carry out on your behalf.

They light up for you the path along which you must journey, in order to be faithful to the consecration which you have made to me. It is a difficult and painful path, marked by many obstacles and threatened by the many snares of my adversary. The Angels take you by the hand and lead you along the path of light, of love and of holiness.

They give you courage and comfort in the many difficulties which you must put up with and they support you in your human weakness. They are at your side as true brothers, who take to heart your person and your life.

They defend you against the continuous attacks of Satan, against his numerous snares, against the obstacles which he puts along your path.

The great battle which is now being waged is above all at the level of the spirits; the wicked spirits against the Angelic Spirits. You are being involved in this struggle which is being waged between Heaven and earth, between the Angels and the demons, between Saint Michael the Archangel and Lucifer. To the Angels of the Lord is entrusted the task of defending your person, the life of the Church and the good of all humanity.

In this great country where you find yourself holding cenacles, you see how humanity, deceived by the false spirits, is going along the way of evil and of a great immorality and how the Church itself is becoming more and more undermined by errors and by sins and is running the danger of losing the true faith, as a result of its division from the Pope and its opposition to his Magisterium.

In these evil times, you must pray much to the Angels of the Lord. *This is the hour of the Angelic Powers.* It is the Angelic Powers who are guiding all my children in the decisive battle for the final defeat of Satan and the coming of the glorious reign of Christ, in the triumph of my Immaculate Heart in the world."

Introduction

Envision in your mind's eye, a pitch black sky. As far as the eye can see, there is not the tiniest glimmer of light. *All is dark!* Then, in an instant, without warning, the entire sky is ablaze with hundreds of thousands[1] of small lights which form a massive sphere of brilliance. The brightness of that light reaches out to every corner of the earth. Gone is the darkness. *All is light!* That is our own vision of how the Angels may have been created. In what is humanly referred to as the blink of an eye, the Angels *were*. God anticipated the creation of man. In His great benevolence, He knew we would need help from above, and so in less than an instant, the Angels were created.

God is so good. He knows how little of our brains we use. We cannot possibly understand His Ways. God knows we could not comprehend the concept of Angels as invisible beings. We have to *see* Angels to understand them. So, for *us*, when they are manifested in human forms[2], He gives them powerful, muscular bodies, with gentle, beautiful feminine faces. He incorporates the best of male and female and puts all of it into one form. He gives them wings, for strength, speed and majesty. But the decision as to whether they have wings, or take on the appearance of cherubs, or mighty soldiers, none of that has anything to do with us. We don't determine it, and it really is not for us to conjecture. God makes those decisions. If *we* decide whether God can give Angels wings, or cannot give them wings, or muscular bodies, or whatever, we limit His power and abilities. And I don't think God is going to put up with too much of that. We cannot lose our perspective of who is the Creator, and who are the created.

---

[1]"myriads upon myriads, thousands upon thousands" Rev 5:11
[2]Gen 18:2-8

There was such an important reason for the creation of Angels. He made them a significant part of our lives. He gave them *power* to help us through this journey to Heaven. They're there by our side at the drop of a hat. And yet, we don't use them. A common expression today is, "*Take the Angels off the unemployment line.*" We have either forgotten about them, lost faith in the ability of the Angels to help us, or are too embarrassed by our peers to mention Angels, fearing we'll be ridiculed as old-fashioned. Many of us have joined the ever-growing number of people searching for a *better mousetrap.* We're in the age of progress; there has to be something better, more powerful, more helpful, in the latest bag of tricks offered us by the world. What our Faith has given us down through the centuries is the same old thing. *But it works! If it isn't broken, don't fix it!*

St. Paul went right to the heart of our belief in Angels, and the battle for our souls, when he warned his followers,

"Put on the armor of God, that you may be able to stand against the wiles of the devil. For our wrestling is not against flesh and blood, but against the Principalities and the Powers, against the world rulers of this present darkness, against the spiritual forces of wickedness on high."[3]

Paul was one of the most brilliant men our Church has ever known. He never wasted words on niceties, when it was important to get to the heart of a subject. But he also didn't go out of his way to antagonize people, unless he had a strong purpose. Why would he make this statement, he, who'd had visions of Heaven, who was so close to Jesus and the Angels, if it were not true? We find it so easy today to dismiss the notion of Angels and devils[4]. We categorize

---

[3]Eph 6:11-12

[4]In a Catholic Commentary, the Scripture Passage "*nor Angels nor Principalities*" in Romans 8:39 is very casually explained away as very possibly 'good or evil spirits'

demons as *psychological.* A Catholic priest, chairman of the Theology department of a major American *Catholic University,*

"dismissed the idea of a personal archdemon as 'premodern and precritical'. Individuals tend to personify evil, 'because we see it in people.' But for sophisticates acquainted with sociology and other disciplines, 'sin is now seen as something systemic, institutional and structural, as well as personal."[5]

Was Paul a seer? Did one of his Angels bring this atrocious attack against our beliefs to Paul, two thousand years ago, so he could warn us (in Ephesians 6: 11-12) about these blasphemies which are so *chic* and *sophisticated* today? Did he know that the day would come when his very words would be contradicted and held up to ridicule by those who are supposed to be on our side? Can you picture St. Paul, one of the most brilliant men our Church has ever known, being reduced to a first century *witch doctor?* What do the illustrious theologians of this final decade of the twentieth century, have to say about St. Augustine, St. Thomas Aquinas, St. Anthony of Padua, St. John of the Cross, St. Bonaventure, and all the other Doctors of the Church, who always admitted to having used the teachings of St. Paul as a basis for their own writings?

Last year, we were giving a talk in a small southern town. The hostess had asked her brother to introduce us. He opened his remarks by saying, *"I like what I read in Bob and Penny Lord's books. I've been to their talks, and they remind me of things my second grade teacher, Sister Mary Regina taught us as children."* We thanked the man for his generous comments, but shared with the group present, we don't mean to talk like Sister Mary Regina did forty years ago, just for the sake of bringing you down the path of

---

[5]Time Magazine, March 19, 1990 - Pg 55

Memory Lane. The only reason, our master of ceremonies mentioned that our comments are reminiscent of something his grade school teacher might have said, is because he doesn't hear these things any more. *And that's sad!* We don't try to bring you back to another time. We're *refocusing* on values that should never have been given up. We're not trying to go backward. We're trying to steel up for what's ahead.

The gifts of power the Lord gave us, and continues to give us, should not be categorized as simply childhood memories. They are current, as modern and touchable as the Word, itself. We are the losers when we allow ourselves to be influenced by *respected scholars* who would put these gifts on the back burner, or infer *mockingly* that they are throwbacks to a less informed, less scientifically based medieval church who needed magic and symbols to survive. Demons have been replaced by *neuroses.* That is certainly Satan's joke. And he's laughing very loudly. If there are no demons, well then, naturally, *there can be no Angels!* Then, is there a God?

But there are so many gifts the Lord has given us, to help us through this journey, this pilgrimage to the Kingdom. And one of the greatest aids we have, is the gift of the Angels. However, very few know anything about them. Don't feel bad. *I never knew anything about them!* Oh, I always knew there were Angels. They have been a part of my Catholic upbringing for as far back as I can remember. I said the Guardian Angel prayer on and off until I was about eight or nine years old. I'm sure the good Nuns told us stories about the Angels in grammar school. But I never really thought anything about Angels. They were there, but they didn't mean anything to me. It took me until I was almost forty years old to realize how important the Angels are, how much power the Lord has given them, and how they are *literally there* to help us get through this pilgrimage of life.

It began on a Labor Day weekend party in 1975. Penny and I went to a friend's house for a barbecue. We had returned to the Church in January of that year, after having left for over three years. Our life was now very exciting. Church was the major focus of everything we did. We surrounded ourselves with members of our Parish, who felt the same way we did about Church, Marriage and Family.

We had gone on a Marriage Encounter weekend in May 1975, which had changed our lives. The very next month, Fr. Chuck Gallagher and 2,000 couples left for a pilgrimage to Lourdes and Rome. Penny and I just couldn't come up with the $500 each it cost to go, and so we missed it. But when they came back and shared the glory, and the majesty, and the excitement of our Church, through their experiences in Lourdes and Rome, Penny and I vowed the next year, we would go on our own pilgrimage, even if we had to hock everything to get the money.

So we really looked forward to this Labor Day party. A cousin of the host had been to Europe, and he was going to tell us about some of the shrines he had visited. He began by sharing about Padre Pio and San Giovanni Rotondo, in Italy. Now, we had never heard of either Padre Pio, or San Giovanni Rotondo, but we listened intently as he explained about this Franciscan Capuchin priest who had the Stigmata of Jesus for fifty years of his priesthood[6]. We were completely overwhelmed by the miracles and spiritual gifts attributed to Padre Pio. So we decided, on the spot, that we would visit San Giovanni Rotondo.

Sort of *as an aside*, the cousin of our host mentioned that just about ten miles from San Giovanni Rotondo was the cave of St. Michael the Archangel. In 490 A.D., Michael had appeared in that cave, and claimed the cave and the

---

[6]We wrote a chapter on Padre Pio in our last book, *Saints and Other Powerful Men in the Church*, and included Padre Pio in a television series we made on that book.

mountain for himself and the Heavenly Hosts of Angels. We will go into more detail on the cave of St. Michael in a later chapter. That was the first mention of an Angel I had heard since my childhood, when Sister Dolores used to tell us stories about the Angels. But I hadn't even thought about Angels since I "*grew up*". After having heard about the cave, Penny and I looked excitedly at each other. We decided we would visit there, too.

Not two weeks later, our pastor, Monsignor Tom O'Connell, asked Penny and me to join him and a group, mostly ladies, to go to the San Fernando Mission church. It was the Holy Year, and we would all get the same blessings if we made a pilgrimage to the Mission church, as if we had been in Rome, at St. Peter's Basilica. So Penny and I jumped at the opportunity. We even brought our eight year old grandson, Rob, with us. It was the first time Rob was an Altar Server. He had always yearned for that gift, and it was given to him that day, *unofficially*.

After the Mass, we were given a tour of this, one of California's famous missions. The tour ended, naturally enough, in the gift shop. I was excited about all the beautiful religious articles there, but I found myself drawn to a little statue of *St. Michael the Archangel*. It took my breath away. It wasn't one of those great Italian alabaster or marble statues. It was a little painted plaster statue, probably made in Spain. But to me, it was the most magnificent image I had ever seen. With the exception of Our Lord Jesus, this was the first time I had ever seen what I would call *a beautiful man!* I couldn't take my eyes off it. He had all the rippling muscles of a powerful man; but his face was soft and gentle, almost feminine. He stood with his sword poised, ready to attack Satan, whose head he was crushing under his feet. His red cape flowed gently around him, and his wings were majestic. He held Satan at bay with such ease.

This was the beginning of my love affair with the Angels. I had to know more about them. I began reading books on the Angels, everything and anything I could get. When Penny and I began our sixteen years of pilgrimages, we visited every shrine known to man, that had anything to do with an Angel. In 1976, we visited the Cave of St. Michael in Italy. In 1977, we visited the Mountain of St. Michael in France. We found out that St. Michael was the Patron Saint of Belgium. It went on and on. I photographed every Angel I could find, from the great Bernini Angels in St. Peter's Basilica, to little cherub Angels in the Church of the Immaculate Conception in downtown Los Angeles.

Little by little, the Lord has been revealing to us the role of the Angels in our lives, the power they have been given by God, how much they want to help us. I like to call the Angels our cousins. I'm not sure if that's Biblical, or liturgically correct, but I feel such a closeness to them, I believe they are directly related to us.

I *need* to feel the power that I know the Lord has given the Angels. I need to feel it in a *physical* way. I love to drive on the highway on a windy, cloudy day, and see what I like to call sculptures in cloud, images of Angels following my car, protecting me. I can see their great wingspan, the majestic flow of their bodies as they move through the sky. We're in a time when hope, morals, all the values we have held dear, are being smashed against the rocks, destroyed, in order to make way for a new world order, a new age that will send us right down to the bowels of hell. I need to *know* that there is strength, there is power, there is hope for me and my family and my church. The Angels, from the sweet little cherubs to the mighty warriors, their muscles rippling, their swords drawn and ready, are just one more way Our Lord tells us loud and clear that *He is in charge; He is with us always; He has not left us orphans.*

We want to share that gift with you. We believe you need it as much as we do, and as much as we want to share it with you. But don't keep it to yourselves. We're in a time when the power and availability of the Angels, to help us get through the rough periods, to counsel and comfort us when we need it, and to finally escort us to meet Our Lord and Our Lady when our time comes, must be shared. You've got to get out there and spread the word. Share some of the stories we're going to tell you in this book.

You know what the most frustrating part of all this is? We have this real urgency to impress on you how powerful the Angels are in our lives. We use all kinds of poetic language to stress this point, but it just doesn't seem to be enough. For those of you who have followed our writings, in the past two years, we have been stressing *power*, the power the Lord gives us. We have written about powerful *men* and powerful *women*; now we're writing about an *Army of Angels*. Can you see the point the Lord is trying to make through all of this? He wants you and me to understand the power He has given us, because we're going to need it, especially in this last decade of the second millennium, what may possibly be the end times.

We don't really expect to fully understand, in our lifetime, the full nature or role of the Angels. But we know what we know. We can feel, deep down inside of us, how crucial it is that we reach out to the Angels *now* for help. The Lord has given them to us; we must use them.

We're in a time when everything we have ever held sacred, is being taken away from us in a very sinister, subtle, organized way. That's the enemy's modus operandi, *subtle* and *sinister*. And we're falling for it. It's crept into our churches, our seminaries, our schools, our homes. We are all becoming victims of a ravenous hunger for knowledge, cleverly packaged for human consumption, with a promise to prove everything beyond a shadow of a doubt, or it does not exist. Faith has gone out the window. *Either prove it or get rid of it.* Tradition is dwindling. *Show it to me on television, or on a printout sheet, a hard copy, or on a digital display.* We're being overpowered by technology.

We're told the concept of Angels is ridiculous. *"Give me a break. Get out of the middle ages. Forget that witchcraft. Get into the twentieth century."* We defend the Angels with the fact that Angels are mentioned in just about every other page of Scripture. We ask, almost afraid of the answer, *"You do believe in Scripture, don't you?"* So the next attack is on Scripture. It's taken Satan two thousand years to build up enough false courage to attack the credibility of Sacred Scripture. But he's out to destroy everything that makes us a church, and a people. The latest heresy is, Jesus didn't say the words that are in the Gospels. *The Gospel writers put the words into his mouth!* Can you understand why we contend it's so important that we have a strong Army to protect us? We're not only getting clobbered from the bad guys, and the world; now we're getting it from the good guys, our own. We pray to the Angels to give us the words to say, that will touch your heart, and compel you to turn in the direction of the Angels, for strength. They function best when they have a strong prayer cover. You must be a prayer warrior to give them the power they need to help you. But before you can do any of that, you must get to know them.

So come with us now. Get to know your cousins, and your very best friends, God's Angels. Find out who they are, what their role in Salvation history has been, how they fit into your life, and form a part of your life, how you can accomplish great things for God and yourself, how you can turn it all around, to the point of being able to change the course of history, by appealing to your Angels for help. Learn how you are not hopeless or helpless. You have strength; you have power; you have family and friends in God's *Heavenly Army of Angels.*

What and who are the Angels?

St. Thomas Aquinas is so outstanding. The Lord has given him the ability to take very complex matters, such as the differences between animal, human and Angel, and break them down into logical, extremely understandable terms. He was particularly enraptured by Angels, as are we. He made a study of them. I have to believe he got a lot of help in his research from the Angels themselves, in the form of Angelic inspiration, or possibly by a direct line.

We pray they will be as kind to us, as we try to explain their culture, and their role in Salvation History in general, and in our lives, more specifically. Strangely enough, it's easier to salute their power and accomplishments, than it is to actually explain them. However, we have an urgency to try. We want you to feel as strongly about them, as close to them as we do, and as in love with them as we are, so you can take advantage of the dominance the Lord has given them on our behalf. They're just waiting for you to ask them to use their strength for you. Sometimes, they don't even wait for you to ask. You know, when something wonderfully impossible has happened to you, it's usually the work of your Angels. If ever there was a time when we needed the Angels, it's now.

The Angels were an immediate creation of God, in His Image and Likeness. The main purpose of their existence is to love and serve God in Heaven, as ours is to love and serve God on earth. In addition, God has given them a whole list of other jobs to perform. In essence, they are *contemplatives in action*. The work they do on behalf of the world and humanity is really an outpouring of the love that comes from being in the Beatific Vision of God. Angels are not human; they are actually superior to man. They might be our big brothers. Scripture tells us we are "*a little less than the Angels*".

In question 50 of his Summa Theologica, Thomas Aquinas gives us an understanding of the substance of Angels, by categorizing the different degrees of existence of *all* creatures. He breaks *creation* down into three groupings, animal, human and Angelic. Animal is completely *body*. Human is a mixture of body with something extra added, a *spirit*. Angels are *pure spirit*, without body at all. "Pure spirit" are the key words here. Because the Angels are pure, they are not corrupted by matter. Therefore, they can't die, or decay, or do anything else that results from being made of matter, like animals and humans. Also, they're not dependent on matter of any kind for their existence. They don't need food to eat, or air to breathe, or water to drink. *They are pure.*

Another exciting thing about the Angels, is that each one is a unique, one of a kind creation of God, like a snowflake. I used to have a problem with this. I didn't quite understand what I was reading. Penny explained it to me. It meant exactly the same as what we tell people about themselves when we give talks. Each of *us* is a unique, one of a kind creation of God. There is no person on earth that is quite like the creation you see when you look in the mirror. The same applies to the Angels.

The only difference is Angels don't have to look in mirrors. They are not burdened down with bodies. This has been a problem for humans from the earliest days, *because we need to see Angels to understand them, and the only way we can see them is if they have bodies.* How can we see Angels with bodies if they don't have them? It's the same as seeing God, the Father, as an old man with white hair and a long white beard, and brilliant white flowing gown. It's a picture we paint of what God might look like, if He were human, and had a body. It's really more for our benefit than it is for Him.

But, we say again, Scripture talks about Gabriel appearing to Mary, and Raphael appearing to Tobias, and Isaac wrestling with the Angel, who may very well have been Michael. *They all had bodies!* We also talk about images of Angels with wings, which have become almost a traditionally accepted form. The most rational explanation for the wings on Angels is their ability to be in so many places so quickly, they have the speed of winged creatures. While that may be true, we have to explain that that is man's logic, his need to break everything down into a human level, put everything in a box, for human understanding. However, it's also putting God in a box, limiting His powers to accommodate our limited intellect.

True, God created Nature, the laws of Nature, and the natural order. It would stand to reason that He would follow the laws He created, and men with wings were not part of what He originally created, as far as we know. Nevertheless, something no one wants to come to terms with is that *God is God!* He is above the laws of Nature that He created. If He wants to change the laws of Nature, or set them aside, or do away with them altogether, He can do that. By the same token, if He wants to give Angels bodies, and put wings on them, for whatever reason, He can. We have to stop trying to bring God down to our level. We were created to glorify God, not to make Him our contemporary, our buddy. We should really go with God's program, rather than insist on constantly questioning it.

Actually, to our way of thinking, Our Lord gave us a very special gift by allowing us to become aware of Angels in the first place, and to see Angels in human form in the second place. It's like getting a peek into Heaven, and things Heavenly. If this is what Angels can be like, what else is up there that we haven't seen yet, and cannot begin to fathom.

Angels were created as pure spirits of God. They were immediately given intellect and knowledge. Nothing happened in degrees. They didn't get a basic understanding, and then build from there. There was no $2+2=4$. It was all there, whatever the Lord wanted them to know. They never had to reason anything out, because there was no need for it. They knew the end of the story right off the bat.

They were created with Sanctifying Grace, but also Free Will. But let's talk for just a minute about Free Will. We have always been under the mistaken impression that Free Will meant we could do whatever we wanted, *do our own thing*, and to a degree, that's true. But that's only a very small part of it. When we were researching Archbishop Fulton J. Sheen for our book, *"Saints and Other Powerful Men in the Church"*, we discovered that Free Will is just the beginning of the definition. We are given Free Will to love and glorify God.

"And there is the freedom of a total abandonment to God: our free will is the only thing that is really our own. Our health, our wealth, our power - all these God can take from us. But our freedom He leaves to us, even in hell. Because freedom is our own, it is the only perfect gift that we can make to God."[1]

As soon as the Angels used this Sanctifying Grace in their first act of charity, which had to be friendship and love of God, they received the Beatific Vision[2]. After this, they were incapable of sinning, because they basked in the presence of God.

But prior to this first act of charity, they were capable of sinning. Because they didn't have bodies, there were only two sins they were capable of committing, *Pride* and *Envy*. And those two sins could only be leveled against God; pride that they could be *as* God, and envy because they could not

---

[1] The World's First Love - Fulton J. Sheen - McGraw Hill 1952

[2] Beatific Vision - The essence of God as seen in the light of glory. This is the essential reward of the blessed in Heaven. Possession of God in the Beatific Vision is man's ultimate happiness.

be God. Lucifer knew that to be equal with God, he would have to be God, and he knew he couldn't be. He wanted to be *like* God, in a way which was impossible; such as creating things on his own power, or achieving the beatific vision without God's help, or to have power over people and things which was reserved for God alone. He wanted to be a parallel god. These were the sins committed by Lucifer and the fallen angels. From that time on, they were responsible for all sin, because they lead men to commit sin.

Angels have been given the tools by God, to perform for Him in whatever way necessary to exalt His Holy Name. They are sent to minister to *His* purposes among creatures. There's an important point. We've been saying from the beginning how Angels are given great powers to help us through this journey of faith, our pilgrimage of life. They have a forceful influence on us. But none of this is because of anything we've done. The Angels are sent to help us because of God's Love for us and their love for God, and their desire to do anything to give Him honor. So when you hear people say, "*Don't be impressed with yourself. God loves you because He loves you, not because of anything you've done to earn it.*" That's the way it is with the Angels.

A perfect example of this is how much our Guardian Angels have to put up with, being in our presence twenty four hours a day, every day of our lives. They fight with us not to do the things we know we shouldn't do. Very often, when temptation comes, and we're either fighting it, or considering whether we're going to give into it, the gnawing in our stomachs is really our Angels trying to influence our decision. Since Angels are superior to man, they can enlighten us. But they can't act directly on our will. They can't hit us over the head with a 2 x 4.

Remember seeing cartoons, as a young person, where the good Angel sits on the right shoulder of the character, trying to get him to do good, and the little demon is on the character's left shoulder, trying to get him to do bad? Possibly, that's an oversimplification of a fact. But brought down to its common denominator, this is just about what happens. Some of those cartoons were *morality* plays.

Very possibly, the most difficult task for the Angels is to have to be present while we're sinning.[3] In the case of Guardian Angels, after they've lost the battle to get us to do good instead of evil, they have to stay there with us while we do whatever evil temptation we've given into. They must be very hurt, not for themselves, but for us, and for their God, Whom they love so completely. They must also be really upset with the fallen angel who was able to talk us into giving in to evil. The good Angel is superior to the fallen angel, but we're the determining factor as to who conquers, good or evil. He's dependent on our using the will power the Lord has given us.[4]

The Roles of the Angels

First off, let's keep in mind that nothing is definite. We will not know the entire story until we have reached the Kingdom, and then it won't matter. There have been disputes as to the number and roles of the various choirs of Angels. Most have accepted three divisions of three, or a total of nine choirs. But there are those who say that there is another one, and others who maintain the total number is eleven. Then, finally, some maintain that we don't know

---

[3]"One day, the Angel looked at her so severely, she began to cry. *'How could you commit such faults in my presence?'* he scolded, his eyes boring a hot coal into her soul." See section on St. Gemma Galgani in chapter - Saints and the Angels, in this book.

[4]It would appear that with some of the Saints, the Guardian Angel remained at all times as in (3), but with others, as St. John Vianney wrote, the Angels removed themselves when the souls in their charge sinned. *"Everyone who enters a ball leaves his Guardian Angel at the door, and a devil takes his place. And so very soon there are as many devils as dancers in the ballroom."* St. John Vianney (Saints and other Powerful Men in the Church)

how many there are.   They claim there are many, many degrees of Angels, whose names we don't know, because of a statement made by St. Paul, *"...high above every principality, power, virtue and domination, and every name that can be given in this age or in the age to come."*[5]   By this, some theologians and early Fathers of the Church believe that St. Paul was telling us there were more than had ever been mentioned.   However, for our purposes, we will share about the accepted number of Angels.

There are three divisions of Angels, called Choirs[6]:

Seraphim, Cherubim, and Thrones -

Angels of this choir's entire existence consists in solely glorifying, loving and praising God.   This is all they do.   Their total energy is focused on praising the Master.   They have such an extremely intense relationship with God, they don't let anything interfere with their adoration.

It's believed that Lucifer, or Satan, had to be in this choir, originally.   He was said to be the closest to God, which would have had to be among the first order or rank of Angels.

Dominations, Virtues and Powers -

These Angels govern Space and the Stars.   They are responsible for the entire universe.   We'd like to insert at this time, a true story, which you may have read before.   It just fits so perfectly with this choir of Angels.

A very holy lady, who has played an important role in our life, Annabel Joyce, from Mission Hills, California, bought a subscription for us to that very special magazine, "*Soul*."   We read the following article in their issue dated May-June, 1986.   Little did we know, at that time, that someday we would be writing a book on the *Angels*.   As we

---

[5]Eph 1:21

[6]Choirs are not meant to be choirs in the sense that we know them. They are really degrees, or ranks, or orders.

began writing this chapter, the Lord, through His Angels reminded us of this article. We telephoned The Blue Army in Washington, New Jersey, and they generously gave us permission to reprint it.

"October 22, 1985, an amazing story appeared in Weekly World News; it reported: Six Soviet cosmonauts aboard the Salyut 7 orbiting space station saw "seven glowing angels" in July of 1985, as their space ship orbited the earth.

This came to light when a Soviet space scientist defected to the West. He brought with him, a top-secret report on the incident.

January 4, 1986, in Parade magazine, a publication which is included with Sunday issues of many newspapers, carried the following:

"Best International News"

"Cosmonauts Vladimir Solevev, Oleg Atkov and Leonid Kizim say they first saw the celestial beings...during their 155th day abroad the orbiting Salyut 7 space station. 'What we saw,' they said, 'were seven giant figures in the form of humans, but with wings and mist-like halos, as in the classic depiction of angels.'"

"What the short account in Parade magazine didn't mention was that the cosmonauts were performing medical experiments in their cramped quarters when a brilliant orange glow enveloped their craft, leaving them temporarily blinded. After their eyes adjusted to the light, they saw the Angels.

"The cosmonauts said the Angels followed their capsule for about ten minutes and then suddenly vanished.

"But twelve days later, the glowing figures returned and were seen by additional Soviet witnesses. Cosmonauts Svetlana Savitskaya, Vladimir Dzhanibevok and Igor

*Volk joined the others on Salyut 7. The woman
cosmonaut was quoted in the above secret report as
saying: 'We were truly overwhelmed. There was a great
orange light and through it we could see the figures of
seven angels. They were smiling as though they shared a
glorious secret. But within a few minutes they were gone
and we never saw them again.'*

*"The soviet defector, who has remained anonymous,
said his countrymen "would prefer to write off the
sightings as hallucinations or some form of unexplained
natural phenomenon. But the evidence seems to
indicate that what they saw was more supernatural that
natural."*

The cosmonauts claimed the Angels were so large, they
had a wing span as wide as a jumbo jet airplane.

*"They were smiling as though they shared a glorious
secret."* What was the glorious secret they shared? Was it
that Russians would once again be free to worship their
Lord and venerate their Mother Mary? Were they smiling
because they knew that the people, the communists had so
long oppressed, would be free, four years later, in December
of 1989? Were they smiling because they knew that someday
the world's faithful would return to their beliefs in God and
the Holy Angels? Were they smiling because they knew
their message would go out to all the world: *You are not
alone. Our Lord has assigned us to you, and we will be with
you till the end*?

This is such an affirmation for us, of the role played by
Dominions, Virtues and Powers.

Principalities, Archangels, and Angels -

This is the area of Angels who are *closest* to us. They
really take care of us. They are in the front lines of the
battlefield, so to speak. Whereas the first group is
steadfastly devoted to praising God, and the second group is

faithfully concerned with the Universe and maintaining the celestial order of things, as God created them, this last rung on the ladder are those who are concerned with their inferior cousins on earth, mankind, and if there should be life on other planets, the welfare of its inhabitants, as well.

They really seem to do all the work. They have to go through all our trials and tribulations with us, our joys and sorrows, our temptations, our illnesses, our clashes with their enemies, the fallen angels. It would appear that the lowest rung of Angels are the only ones who have actual contact with their adversaries, the fallen angels of Satan, because they are the only ones concerned with man.

Our Holy Angels are also given the task of protecting countries, cities, and churches. It has always been believed that this was so, but the vision of the Prophet Daniel was what really affirmed their role. There's also an interesting lesson for us in the happenings of that vision.

The nations involved are Israel, Persia and Greece. We find that Michael is the Angel protector of Israel, Gabriel of Greece, and an unnamed Archangel the Angel Protector of Persia. It was the time of the Persian imprisonment of the Jews. The Prophet Daniel beseeched the Archangel Gabriel to help in the release of the Jews from the Persians. Gabriel turned the matter over to Michael, and the two solicited the aid of the Angel Protector of Persia, *but he refused.*

The reason, we are given, is that each Angel Protector was completely involved in the interests of his own country. The Angel Protector of Persia had noticed how the presence of the Israeli people had changed the Persians, bringing many blessings and conversions to this pagan people. He, most naturally, wanted to keep the Jews in captivity longer, as this was bringing Persians to God. From his perspective, all he could see was the good being accomplished for his nation by the captivity of the Jews.[7]

With regard to Angels being protectors of churches, it was logical that if the Lord gave Angels the job of protecting nations, they would also have the job of protecting churches. But if there was any doubt to that, it was cleared up by the opening of the Book of Revelation, where St. John was directed to address his letters to the Angels of the Seven Churches of Asia Minor. *"This is the secret meaning of the seven stars you saw in my right hand, and of the seven lampstands of gold; the seven stars are the presiding spirits (Angels) of the seven churches, and the seven lampstands are the seven churches.[8]"*

In *Belgium*, they claim Michael as the patron Saint of their nation.

In *Portugal*, when the Angel appeared to the children: Lucia, Francisco and Jacinta, he called himself the Angel of Peace. This is one of the titles given to Michael. In addition, the Angel of Portugal is called the Angel of Peace.[9]

In *France*, in Mont St. Michel, a place considered the eighth wonder of the world, the Angel Michael came and claimed a forest for his very own.[10]

In *Italy*, the Angel Michael claimed a mountain for his own.[11]

In the *United States*, one of her largest cities, Los Angeles, California, is named after the Angels and their Queen Mary: *La Reina de Los Angeles de la Portiuncola*.

You might ask, how, if these places are under the protection of the Angels, is there so much violence, wars and terrorism. Again, the gift, the Lord has given us, of *free will*.

---

[7]Daniel Chapter 10 & 11
[8]Rev 1:20
[9]see chapter on *Fatima and the Angel* in this book.
[10]written in detail in chapter on the Angels apparition
[11]See Chapter on *St. Michael's Cave and Mountain*

Our Guardian Angel is always there, as the prayer to the Guardian Angel says, "*to light and guard, to rule and guide.*" But, like our Gentle Savior, he does not force himself on us. We have to say *yes.*

More dangerous than any spirit or fallen angel is the human who says *yes* to him. The fallen angels are helpless to do anything without our consent. And so, the same applies with the good Angels. This is the way God created us and them.

It takes a great deal of studying the Scriptures, of putting one passage with another, to understand in the slightest bit, the role and character and number of our cousins, the Angels. But we'll never really know any of this, and we shouldn't concern ourselves over who outranks who, or who might be more important than another. St. Dionysus, who did extensive study on the Angels, wrote,

"*I hold that none but the Divine Creator, by whom they were ordained, is able to know fully the number and the nature of the celestial Beings and the regulation of their Hierarchies....We could not have known the mystery of these super celestial Intelligences and all the holiness of their perfection had it not been taught to us by God through His ministers who truly know their own natures. Therefore we will say nothing as from ourselves, but being instructed we will set forth, according to our ability, those Angelic visions which the venerable theologians have beheld.*"

We should just thank God that He has given us these Heavenly relatives to help us get through the pilgrimage of life. St. Thérèse of Lisieux characterized us as "*pilgrims in a foreign land*", trying to find our way Home. The Angels are there to guide us in the right direction. Thank You, Lord.

Above: ***Three Angels visit Abraham and predict the birth of his
son, Isaac Gen 18:2-8***
Below: ***The Cherubim ejects Adam and Eve from the Garden
of Eden Gen 3:24***

The Angels Bridge the Gap

In the history of the world, there have *always* been great gaps, separators which isolate one land mass from another. As a result of these natural boundary lines, countries have been formed; ethnic cultures have developed; physical and social separation were created. Whether mountains or rivers, or lava from a volcano spewing out a separating line of black rock, or a crack in the earth severing the terra firma deep into its core, from an ancient earthquake too violent to be measured on the Richter scale, the bottom line results have always been the same, complete and utter division.

The religions of the world have not been spared from this inundation of separativeness. The earthquake that occurred on that first Good Friday, after Jesus had uttered His last cry, *"Father, into Thy Hands I commend My Spirit"*, tore apart the curtain in the temple, and fractured the temple area. The rumble from that outrageous act of murder against the Body of the Son of God could be felt around the world. It caused a split high up on a mountain in Italy, called Alverna, at the moment of Jesus' death[1]. This same mountain is where St. Francis of Assisi received the wounds of the Stigmata, some twelve hundred years later.

Perhaps a worse crack formed when the Christians split from the Jews. Granted, it was a spiritual or emotional fissure, but a devastating break nevertheless. Originally, it was clean; deep, but clean. The Jews would not accept Our Lord Jesus as their Messiah. That was it, pure and simple, the only line of separation. Other than that, everything about the *new way* of Jesus was on a parallel with Judaism. Christians even went to the temple to worship; *then* they

---

[1]According to Franciscan tradition

would gather together at someone's home to break bread, and share about the Messiah. This is the ancient beginnings of our Mass.

But when the Jews refused to accept Jesus as their Messiah, the Gentiles were evangelized and converted. Changes began to work their way into the Christian religion, and away from the Mosaic laws, (i.e. circumcision and some Kosher dietary laws)[2] causing the gap to widen and deepen, until eventually, it became too wide and too deep, too impossible for humans to cross without help. As time went on, it took more than accepting Jesus as the Messiah for a Jew to join the Christian movement. There were Jewish laws which had nothing to do with the teachings of Jesus, and so they were not observed. This was something Jews who had joined the church, could not obey; at first they fought and then they left.

And so separation came about! This separation was obviously a plan of the evil one to form a deep and permanent gap between Jews and Christians, which was never meant to be. Jesus had come for His chosen people the Jews, dying for them as well as those who would come later, the Gentiles. Lucifer's plot was designed for Jews and Christians to kill one another, eventually destroying the Church.

But it does seem strange that the perpetrators of the plot, the fallen angels, should have failed to consider the one entity, God had made strong enough to foil that plot, to bridge that gap, to cross that great chasm separating the old and the new, without fear of falling deep into the ravine, *was their brothers*, the good Angels. This bridge would stand for all time, as Jesus stood on the other side of the water, waiting for His beloved people to cross over to Him and His Church.

---

[2]Acts 11:1-18

Angels have been a major factor in the Judaeo-Christian tradition, from the very beginning. While Bible Scholars of different Christian denominational persuasions disagree on just about everything in Scripture, as do our brothers and sisters of the Hebrew belief, there has always been one area where there has never been a disagreement, and that is the Biblical recognition of the authenticity and role of the Angels.

That Angels bridge the gap between the Old Testament and the New Testament is a well-known fact. Their existence and activities can be traced as far back as Genesis, and continue up through the Book of Revelation, the last book of the Bible, where they play a major part in the prophecy of the endtimes. Through Scripture, we see their roles as varied, as are their powers and charisms. Because of these special qualities of leadership, we believe the Angels have distinct personalities, to perform individual tasks. But no matter how we view the Angels personally, they are always there in Scripture, at crucial times, and they play important roles. *They are right up there standing in attendance with God.*[3]

The Angels themselves are mentioned no less than 320 times in the Old and New Testaments, as well as, in every *main* event in the Life of Jesus. The Angels are mentioned in the Garden of Eden. After the expulsion of Adam and Eve, God put Cherubim as guards of the gates of Eden. *"He drove out the man; and at the east of Eden He placed the Cherubim, and the flaming sword, which turned every way, to guard the way to the tree of life."*[4]

By the time Adam and Eve were thrown out of the Garden of Eden, the battle between the good Angels and the followers of Lucifer, had already been fought and

---

[3]Luke 1:19
[4]Gen 3:24

decided. Lucifer was given the form of *the serpent*[5]. So even then, before what we humans consider *the dawn of creation*, battle lines had been drawn. Sides had been taken; roles had been allocated; the good Angels trying to help man; the fallen angels trying to destroy man. But even that early in the game, it was very obvious that man was just a tool, a scorecard in the hands of Satan, to show God how powerful *he* was, and what a waste of God's time mankind was.

The Angels were appointed right from the beginning, by God Himself, to watch over us, to guide and protect us.

"For to His Angels He has given command about you, that they guard you in all your ways.

"Upon their hands they shall bear you up, lest you dash your foot against a stone.

"You shall tread upon the asp and the viper; you shall trample down the lion and the dragon."[6]

Although these words from the Psalms, are prophecy of the Angels' protection first and foremost to our Lord Jesus, they are no less meant for us, His children.

Our Faithful God promised His chosen people *protection* for their long journey from Egypt to the Promised Land:

"See, I am sending My Angel before you, to guard you on the way and bring you to the place I have prepared."

But Loving and All-Wise Father, He also warned them:

"Be attentive to him and heed his voice. Do not rebel against him, for he will not forgive your sin. My authority resides in him. If you heed his voice and carry out all I tell you, I will be an enemy to all your enemies and a foe to all your foes."[7]

"My authority resides in him." The Lord's authority *resides* in His Angels! When we know that our Angel is

---

[5]Gen 3:14
[6]Ps 91:11-13
[7]Ps 23:20

guiding us to go one way and we choose the other path, we are not only defying him, but God Himself! *Defy God Himself?* When I believed with the mind of a child, I used to think the God of the Old Testament was an angry, punishing God who wasn't very loving. As I began to grow up *spiritually*, I began to recognize how involved He has always been in His people's lives, always faithful even in their unfaithfulness. He was always with them, never leaving them alone, even when they rejected Him and tried to block Him out of their lives. Always loving, He was ready to take them back, like the father of the prodigal son. That's when I realized the God of the Old and the New Testament were of One Heart and one Mind. Father and Son and Holy Spirit in One God, One Love.

God, our Father, the One Who created us, knows us *perfectly*; He knows what makes us happy, what is best for us. He does not punish us here on earth; we punish ourselves. We suffer because we go against His Will; His Plan for us is peace and joy. Throughout Salvation History, God sent His Messengers to help us live in this world.

In the *Old Testament*, Angels appeared to humans seventeen times. Although the Old Testament does not refer specifically to Guardian Angels, there is no doubt who accompanied *Jacob* on his journey: "*While Jacob was going on his way, Angels of God encountered him, and on seeing them he said, 'This is God's Camp...*"[8] Travel was perilous in those days. Terrorism is not a new thing, but a very demonic and old horror. It was especially necessary then, as it is now, to have the protection of the Angels.

As the Lord sent His Angels to accompany and lead His people out of Egypt, freeing them from slavery, so He did once more with *Judith*, a Jewish woman who would free her people once again from captivity, only now from another

---

[8]Gen: 32:1

tyrant. She definitely needed the strength and the cover of the Angels to be able to subdue and slay the powerful and dreaded Holfernes, general of King Nebuchadnezzar's army.

In the *New Testament*, Angels appear thirteen times, the first one to Zechariah[9], announcing the birth of John the Baptist, and the last in the Book of Revelation[10], as the Angels of the seven churches of Asia Minor. Angels are described as Spiritual beings, created beings, a *Heavenly Army*, immortal, holy, innumerable, wise, powerful, of the elect, obedient, possessing emotions, invisible. Peter tells us they are concerned with human affairs[11]; we know that, at times, Angels have taken human form, as when they visited Sara and Abraham, and predicted the birth of their son Isaac, just before they destroyed Sodom and Gomorrah[12].

Angels have very definite roles, where it concerns the children of God, in that they are supposed to guide us, direct us, provide for us, protect us, deliver us, direct our activities, comfort us in time of sorrow, and minister to us in time of need. They have been known to be the voice of our consciences. They also have very clearly defined jobs with regard to the enemies of God. They destroy, curse, persecute, kill, cause pestilence and sudden death.[13] This could all be put under the category of "*Smite*". God used Angels often to smite. And while it's true that most of this took place in the Old Testament, there are some accounts in the New Testament, especially in the Book of Revelations, where the Angels put on their heavy armor to do battle with the enemies of God.

However, in the New Testament, for the most part, Angels were involved with the life and Ministry of Jesus.

---

[9]Lk 1:11-20
[10]Rev 1:20
[11]1 Pet 1:12
[12]Gen 18:2-8
[13]from Dictionary of the Bible by John L. Mckenzie,S.J.

They were still very protective, but they seemed to take on more of a gentle nature, consoling Jesus in the Garden of Gethsemane, caring for the women of Jesus: accompanying our sweet Mother Mary on her lonely walk without her Son, rolling back the stone when Mary Magdalene and the other women who were with her, went to the tomb of Jesus. The Angels were active in protecting the Apostles as a group, as well as Peter, Philip, Cornelius, Paul and of course, John, author of the Book of Revelation, individually.

There are so many things we learn about the Angels from Scripture. But, do we pay attention to them? For instance, do you have any idea how *big* an Angel can be? When the Jews were being led out of Egypt, the Lord sent *an* Angel, referred to as *The* Angel. It would seem like we're talking about *one* Angel here, to handle the entire nation of Israel. The Angel took the form of a cloud, which covered the whole group. How big did that Angel have to be?

Also, as we mentioned in a previous chapter, in 1985, Russian cosmonauts were in a space station, when they all claimed to have seen Angels in Space, following their ship. They smiled at the cosmonauts all the time they followed them. They were *huge*, according to the cosmonauts. *They had the wingspan of a 747!*

Strangely enough, in this world of materialism and selfishness, of *"If I don't see it, I don't believe it,"* Angels still occupy a significant and definite place in our *uncelestial* society. In the secular world, the world of commercialism, Angels are used to portray characters *"a cut above."* Television uses *Angels* to give products that extra *special* connotation. Angels are depicted as both provincial and sophisticated. Books, movies and Broadway plays often use Angels in their plots. Movies describe humans who are extra special, as *"Almost Angels."* Everyone has heard the song, *"I married an Angel."* A few years back, there was a television series on prime time in which Michael Landon played an Angel working on earth.

There is a very definite mystique surrounding the Angels. Most people don't really know *how* they look upon Angels, other than, they are *special*, and can be counted on to help. And yet, the most outrageous, most unbelievable thing we can say is, there are those, some of which are in our own dear Church, who would reduce the Angels to mythological creatures.

The Angels are Universal

We didn't actually consider *Angels as Universal*, until we began writing this chapter. Angels have been used by God to be instruments, not only to bridge the gap between the Old and the New Testament, but between the secular and religious world.

We were shocked, in 1991, during the Persian Gulf War, when Saddam Hussein told his troops that the Angels were protecting them. We wanted to cry out, "*But the Angels belong to us! They're on our side.*"

But, now I wonder if the war did not end, as quickly as it did, without the carnage and loss of life threatened by Saddam Hussein, because of the hundreds of thousands of mothers and fathers, sisters and brothers, wives, husbands and children who were praying their loved ones, on both sides, *Allied and Iraqi*, be spared! We have said, the Angels need our prayers to spur them into action. Well, even an American general, General Schwarzkopf, gave credit to the Lord's intercession, calling the end of the war, with the incredibly small number of casualties, a *Miracle*! Did the Angels of both sides get together and do what was impossible for man to do? What do you think? I *know*, in my heart, and nothing can change that.

The Angels are *universal*. They are really non-denominational, non-sectarian. No one religion can claim them exclusively, and yet all religions can embrace them. The way there are Angel Protectors for countries and cities and churches, there are most likely Angel Protectors for religions as well, who, at some given point before the last days, will carry out God's command to bring everybody back to the Holy Trinity, God the Father, God the Son, and God the Holy Spirit. We believe He will use this near perfect form, His Angels, as He has since before the beginning of time, to bridge the gap again, bringing everyone back to Jesus. *It's so exciting! God is so smart!*

✝

Act of Consecration
to Saint Michael the Archangel

Oh most Noble Prince of the Angelic Hierarchies, valorous warrior of Almighty God, and zealous lover of His glory, terror of the rebellious angels, and love and delight of all the just ones, my beloved Archangel Saint Michael, desiring to be numbered among your devoted servants, I, today, offer and consecrate myself to you, and place myself, my family, and all I possess under your most powerful protection.

I entreat you not to look at how little I, as your servant, have to offer, being only a wretched sinner, but to gaze, rather, with favorable eye at the heartfelt affection with which this offering is made, and remember that if from this day onward I am under your patronage, you must during all my life, assist me, and procure for me the pardon of my many grievous offenses and sing, the grace to love with all my heart, my God, my dear Savior Jesus, and my Sweet Mother Mary, and obtain for me all the help necessary to arrive to my crown of glory.

Defend me always from my spiritual enemies, particularly in the last moments of my life.

Come then, oh Glorious Prince and help me in my last struggle, and with your powerful weapon cast far from me into the infernal abyses that prevaricator and proud angel that one day your prostrated in the celestial battle.

Saint Michael defend us in our daily battle so that we may not perish in the last Judgment.

Santuario S. Michele Arcangelo - Monte St. Angelo, Italy

Left:
*Statue of Guardian
Angel at Our Lady of
the Angels Monastery,
Birmingham, Alabama*

Below:
*Bob and Penny Lord
with Mother Angelica at
Eternal Word Television
Network*

The Guardian Angels

Angel of God
My Guardian dear
To Whom His love
Commits me here
Ever this day
Be at my side
To light and guard
To rule and guide.
Amen

In Italy, in my grandparent's day, when a baby was born of the aristocracy, a child was chosen to be his or her companion for life. When my grandmother was born, such a girl-child became her companion. When grandmother grew up and married, the companion went with her to America. After they arrived in the *New World*, although my grandparents released her from any obligation to remain with them, she stayed with them until she died, and is buried in a plot between my grandmother and grandfather.

Our Church teaches us that at birth we are given a Companion who will remain with us until the day we die, then continues with us, even to visiting us in Purgatory to console us in between his trips to our loved ones, pleading with them to pray for us. This Companion, whom we call our *Guardian Angel* faithfully stays by our side right up to the day, his work done, he presents us at the entrance of the Kingdom of God.

Angels Unaware

There are many stories that can be told of a *mysterious voice* warning you of danger, of something or was it *someone interfering* in the knick of time. As we started to write this book on Angels, we found ourselves remembering incidents in our lives we had long forgotten. Could it be our Guardian Angels reminding us? Why not?

Penny and her Guardian Angel on the Road

Many years ago, when our children were very young, Bob and I decided to bring them and my mother on a tour of the Southeastern part of the United States. We thought we could incorporate a vacation with business, by selling merchandise to retail stores, as well.

We lived on Long Island, in New York, at the time. The night we began our journey, Bob had to remain behind. He would join us in a couple of days. I had been up for about 17 hours, when we set out for Washington, D.C. I was so excited to be bringing our family on this holiday, I was not sleepy. Besides, I thought there would be less traffic on the highway at night, and I could make better time.

My family and I arrived in Washington D.C. early in the morning. I left my mother and two children at a very pleasant family-type motel where they could swim and relax, until I returned from calling on my two accounts. The only problem was, the two accounts were department stores in *Richmond, Virginia*, about 150 miles from Washington, D.C., and I had to see the buyers in the daytime hours; so, I set out without resting. I worked until 7 in the evening. When I left Richmond to return to Washington, I had been up, without sleep, for 36 hours.

Not even stopping to have a cup of coffee or a bite to eat, eager to return to my family (as I was sure my mother would be worried), I got in my car and began the long drive back to Washington, D.C. I was not aware I *had fallen asleep* until I'd hear a sharp commanding voice call me by my baptismal name: *Pauline!* I would snap my head upright and swerve my car to the right, just as I was about to collide *head-on* with a huge Mack truck coming straight at me from the other side of the highway.

This went on for hours, over and over again, because I was too much of a fool to even stop to get a cup of coffee. I'd fall asleep, and a voice would sharply awaken me, just in the nick of time. Not having been brought up with knowledge of the Angels and in particular my Guardian Angel, I could not explain it. I just knew someone kept waking me up, calling me by a name I had not used in years. While we were researching this book, I found a passage which explains to me what had happened during that trip. *"They (Angels) protect our spiritual and corporal bodies...They often shield us from sudden dangers that threaten our lives, or come to our rescue when some harm has befallen us."*[1]

I now believe it was my *Guardian Angel.*

"And the Angel who talked with me
came again, and waked me,
like a man that is awakened out of his sleep."
(Zech4:1)

The Angels and the Rosary

How many times, *Dear Friends*, have you been there to save us, even from ourselves? Bob and I were still in the business world. On this particular day, I was receiving some very upsetting phone calls from customers and manufacturers. Time came for me to pick up my grandson from high school; he was not old enough to drive. As I drove toward his school, I became concerned that the anger that had invaded my heart and soul might spread to my boy. Seeking peace, as only the Lord and His Mother can provide, I prayed the Rosary for a half hour, right up to the parking lot of his school.

Rob (my grandson) got in the car, and we then tried to get onto the freeway. I was in the far right lane trying to merge into traffic. I could barely squeeze into the *slow* lane on my left. Cars were barely moving. Finally, having entered

---

[1]Beyond Space - Pg. 126

it, I tried to get into the faster lanes, to no avail. I was blocked in: first by the car in front, then by the car in the rear, and then by the car on the left who would not move up and give me room to get in, no matter how much I flashed my left-turn signal. Well, this was not helping my former attitude a bit. Now, I was really getting *upset*!

Suddenly, I felt the car go out of control! I tried to steer the wheel; it was locked! I shot out my right arm to block my grandson from going through the window. I shouted, "*No, Lord, not him.*" The car stopped dead! My foot started to shake. It was still on the brake which had not worked. I had tried to push the brake pedal through the floor board. When my trembling had subsided, I got out of the car on my side. On Rob's side, we were on the edge of a precipice about forty feet above the road below.

A highway patrolman came to our aid. He shook his head and said there was no earthly reason why we were not dead. The tow truck arrived. The driver used some expletives, I will not repeat, and shook *his* head as he helped us into the cab of his tow truck. Our car was helplessly raised in the air behind us. When we arrived at the gas station, the mechanic dialed the phone for me. I burst into tears, as I tried to tell Bob what had happened. I really didn't know myself.

The mechanic later told Bob if Rob and I were not standing there in front of him, and if the highway policeman had not verified the story, he would not have believed it. He showed us how the axle had snapped in two, severing the wheel from the rest of the car. The wheel should have spun off; we and the car should have capsized and plunged into the road and the cars below. Instead, it became *wedged* in the fender, and prevented the car from moving and turning over. No one could explain it at the time. They had never seen anything like it. It was as if *someone* had jammed the wheel, bracing the car.

Was that an Angel who had wedged the wheel beneath the car? Were they Angels who blocked my path, and locked me in the right lane, not allowing us to go into the fast lane? If we had been in the fast lane, we would have been going so fast, not only would *we* have died but we would have taken other lives with us. There would definitely have been a pile-up. Maybe it was someone else's Angel who interceded. Maybe it was the Guardian Angel of someone who would discover the cure for Cancer.

Or could it be, it was that God heard my cry and called upon our Guardian Angels to save my grandson? Or was it the Queen of Angels to whom I had been praying the Rosary before I picked up my grandson. Had *She* summoned her army of Angels? After all, our grandson had always loved her. He had been in the Junior Legion of Mary when he was a little boy. Did she have a special plan for him?

Or was it because one day the Lord would fill us with the desire to write about Him, His Mother, His Saints and now the Angels? Were the fallen angels upset? Did they not want you to know you are not alone? Was there another battle between the good Angels and the fallen angels being waged? Did the good Angels block the fallen ones from trying to prevent us from doing God's work? I don't know; your guess is good as mine. But the Angels were there; you can count on that.

An encounter with an Angel at the airport

Years ago, when we were just beginning our Party Goods manufacturing business, Bob and I did everything; as the expression goes, we were *chief cook and bottle washer*. I was the only salesperson, besides Bob. I did most of the traveling, selling to department stores around the country, while Bob remained in New York, supervising the plant, calling on New York accounts and caring for our family.

Our cash flow was so poor, I didn't dare return home without orders. We needed them not only to pay our help but little things like rent, telephone bills and groceries for our family. When you start a business with more ideas than money, you live from day to day and hand to mouth. As I wrote an order, I'd telephone Bob long distance and he would ship it out. In that way, the company factoring[2] our accounts would advance the money we desperately needed to cover our overhead.

On one particular trip, I was getting ready to return home when I got caught in a blizzard in Detroit, Michigan. The trip had been longer than most and I was not only tired, but now with the devastating news that the airport was closed, and all flights delayed, that our plane could not land no less take off on time, I was at the point of tears. But forever the optimist, I decided to not only remain in the airport awaiting the next flight to New York, but I waited at the *gate*. I was sure the next notice on the board would be that my plane had arrived, and we would be taking off within the hour.

Even as hours slowly ticked away into more hours, into finally 3 in the morning, I couldn't leave that spot. I just *knew* the plane would be arriving any moment. Suddenly, something or was it *someone* seemed to awaken me. I hadn't realized I had fallen asleep. I shot up sharply from the huddled position I was in. As my glasses had fallen off, the figures coming toward me were kind of hazy; they looked as if they were weaving. I put on my glasses and realized it wasn't my poor eyesight; the two men staggering toward me had not been spending their waiting hours praying, but drinking.

The only traveling I had ever done, *alone*, was when I went to college. Now years later, here I was and I was

---

[2]Loaned us money on orders we had shipped

petrified! Traveling alone so unnerved me that when checking into a hotel, I would always ask for a room next to the elevator. I had never shared these fears with Bob because, no matter how needed the orders were for us to survive, he would never have allowed me to go out of town. And now, my worst fears were to be realized!

I froze! I wanted to scream; but as there seemed to be no one else around, who would hear me? Part of me felt foolish, but the other part of me was saying *run!* I couldn't move! I kept telling my mouth to open and scream, but it wouldn't listen. My legs seemed to have a mind of their own, as well, and wouldn't cooperate anymore than my voice. *Lord, help me.* The two drunks were making lewd and lecherous comments.

Suddenly from another direction, a man appeared. My first thought was, *Oh Lord, not another one.* He came over to me and sat about five feet away. He started to speak to me with the gentlest voice. He never came any closer, but he evidently discouraged the other two men, as they soon walked away. He stayed with me right up to and including boarding the plane. He did not leave me until he got off at his city.

Had my guardian Angel called him? Was he my Guardian Angel? Did my Guardian Angel take on human form to try to console and protect me? I remember the man till today. He was blonde; his hair was thinning a little. He was slightly built. He had the kindest blue eyes. He had a great sense of humor and was able to laugh at himself. He told me he was a minister in the Pentecostal Church. My fear gone, I became my own *bull in a china shop* self and I blurted out, "*Oh, I thought all Pentecostals were loud, pew and floor thumping holy rollers[3]. You're so soft spoken. You don't*

---

[3]Holy rollers- a slang name used years ago for members of the Pentecostal church.

seem to fit the description." He laughed, as he told me a little about himself, assuring me that not all Pentecostals shouted and waved their arms. Just as my Jesus has come to me, so many times over the years, in different forms, ages, color and sizes, why not an Angel? Did my Angel take the form of a *Pentecostal minister?*

Mother Angelica and her Guardian Angel

As you drive up to EWTN, you immediately become aware of the Angels and their Queen. Right in front of the Blessed Sacrament Chapel an Army of Angels is posted on a hill, honoring Mother Mary and protecting Mother Angelica, her Nuns, the Monastery and her Apostolate, The Eternal Word Television Network. Even the truck containing her portable studio, including a satellite uplink, that EWTN uses to go on-site to bring us so much of their fine programming, is named after the Angel *Gabriel*.

When we first began delving into Mother Angelica's story, we wondered how a little girl with so little to live for became the powerful woman she is, today. As we studied more about her, we discovered the strong place the *Angels* have always played in her life.

To the eyes of the foolish, it would have appeared she was alone much of the time. When we wrote one part of her story, in particular, we could see how, like the Prophets before her, the Lord had a plan and He never left her alone until that plan was fully executed. Thank God, she and He are not finished, yet.

"With no earthly father to watch over her, Rita (Mother Angelica) was to have the love and watchful care of The Father, our Lord and Savior. One day, as a young girl, when crossing a heavily trafficked street, tired and a little distracted, she did not see an oncoming automobile until it was too late to avoid the speeding, fatal impact. She closed her eyes, waiting for the worst, when she felt hands

lifting her up. Upon opening her eyes, she discovered herself standing on the median, safe and untouched. It was her first experience with the protective love of her Guardian Angel. The bus driver who witnessed the event, later recounted the story to Mae (Mother Angelica's mother). He said it was as if Rita leaped in the air, or had been hurled high above the car and onto the median."[4]

Padre Pio and the Guardian Angels

Padre Pio would ask Padre Agostino to stay with him during some of his ecstasies. As he was having ecstasies, Padre Agostino would hurriedly try to jot down Padre Pio's words. He said that Padre Pio's Angel would laugh as Padre Pio playfully teased him. This is an excerpt from one of Padre Pio's ecstasies recorded by Father Agostino. It's dated November 29, 1911. You can see that Padre Pio and his Guardian Angel were like two very close friends. My Bob only teases people he trusts. And so, it is obvious Padre Pio trusted his Angel enough to kid with him.

"...Angel of God, my Angel...Are you not taking care of me?...Are you a creature of God?...Either you're a creature of God or a creator...You're a creator? No? Therefore you are God's creature and you must have laws which you must obey...You must stay beside me whether you want to or not...He laughs...what is there to laugh about? Tell me one thing...who was here yesterday morning?...He laughs...an Angel laughs!...Tell me ...I won't leave you until you tell me..."

"If not, I will ask Jesus...and then you'll catch it!" Padre Pio turns to Mother Mary. She laughs. Seeing he is getting nowhere fast, Padre Pio turns to Jesus..."*Jesus, You tell me.*" Father Agostino assumes

---

[4]an excerpt from the chapter: "Mother Angelica Alive"-*Saints and other Powerful Women in the Church.*

the Angel answers Padre Pio because he says, *"It took a lot for you to say it, little man."*

As close as he was with his Guardian Angel, so he was under constant attack from the fallen angels. During one of his ecstasies, Father Agostino heard him say,

"Jesus, will the evil one come tonight? Well, help those who assist me, protect them and defend them." (Padre Pio is referring to the friars, he would ask to stay with him, at times to help him ward off the onslaught of the fallen angels.) He continues, *"I know you are there...but Angel of mine, stay with me!"*

Padre Pio would always tell his spiritual children to send their Guardian Angels to him. Then he would complain that *their* Angels kept him up all night.[5]

Pope John XXIII and the Guardian Angels

Angelo Roncalli, known to the world as Pope John XXIII, the rotund little man who was supposed to be an *"interim Pope"*, but wound up being responsible for changing the Church as we know it today, had an unbelievable devotion to the Angels, especially his Guardian Angel. He never had a problem talking about the Angels, not only to his priests and bishops, but to non-Catholics and non-Christians for that matter.

Pope John XXIII had more to say about his Guardian Angel than anyone in the Church, with possible exception of Padre Pio. John XXIII encouraged familiarity with the Guardian Angel. *"Get to know him. Talk to him. He will answer you."* This Pope was a very simple man. He took the Lord's words at face value. There was never in his mind, any question regarding the existence of Guardian Angels or their role in the lives of humans. It came from the Word of God, and that was good enough for him. He didn't argue the fact. He didn't try to blow the Angels out of proportion, or make

---

[5]"Send Me Your Guardian Angels" - Fr. Alessio Parente

them into something they were not. They were important *enough*; their role in salvation history was overwhelming.

He used every opportunity he could to expound on the Guardian Angels, especially how they were working in the world during his time. He encouraged parents to teach their children about Guardian Angels.

"Parents should teach their children that they are never alone, that they have an Angel at their side, and show them how to have a trusting conversation with this Angel." On another occasion, he said, *"Your Guardian Angel is a good adviser; he intercedes near God, on your behalf; he helps us in our needs; he protects us from dangers and accidents. The Pope would like the faithful to feel the wonderful help the Angels give."*

Send your Guardian Angel

We can send our Guardian Angel to link wings with the wings of the Guardian Angels of loved ones, encircling them, protecting them from danger. If our loved ones are in danger of being hurt physically, spiritually, mentally or emotionally, we can send our Guardian Angel to speak to the Angel of the person who could hurt them. Either the two Angels could join together to block that person from hurting our loved ones, or to talk to him to convince him not to harm them.

John XXIII was the greatest proponent of having your Guardian Angel appeal to the Guardian Angel of another person that you may be having difficulty with. Very often, when he was preparing to go to a meeting with someone or *someones* he knew to be antagonistic, he would call upon his Guardian Angel to speak to the Guardian Angel of his adversary, and soften his heart. He could not recall how many times this had changed the course of some very important meetings.

Pope John XXIII also gave credit to his Guardian Angel for the inspiration of convening Vatican Council II. He claimed always, to pray to Our Lord through his Guardian Angel. He believed sincerely that his Guardian Angel brought him the message from Jesus for Vatican II.

Bring my husband back to me

There was a famous television personality who, one day, told his wife he was leaving her. There was no other woman, he said, but he didn't want to be married any longer. She cried. She pleaded, but all to no avail. Good solid Christian friends told her she must pray, to remember that Jesus abhors divorce! She was to live her life as if her husband would come through the door the next moment. Believing, praying and hoping, she persevered as the months turned into almost two years. There was no sign of her husband coming back. The gossip columns and scandal magazines were having a party!

Often alone in her home, (or was she alone) she could barely keep from running out and *making a life for herself.* Then one night, she answered the door and who do you think was standing before her? Her husband! He asked her if he could come back home, if she would take him back. He said, he didn't know what happened to him, but all of a sudden, he was sitting in a restaurant and he had this irresistible urge to return to her and his home. Not only have they reconciled, but they are actively giving testimony on the power and hope of prayer. Who put that thought into his mind and that desire into his heart? Could it be Guardian Angels at work?

We can send our Angel to summon someone to Church.

One day, in Little Rock, Arkansas, there was a Healing Service to be given by Father Ralph Di Orio. But before it began, the Bishop of Little Rock processed into the Arena with the Blessed Sacrament. As he passed by and raised the

Blessed Sacrament, blessing the people, you could hear "*I can walk. I can hear. I can see.*" People were throwing away crutches, rising from wheel chairs. There were those who began to hear and see with the eyes of the heart as well as those of the body: healings of hurts and painful memories were taking place. The faithful sought reconciliation, forming long lines to have their confessions heard. There was an air of peace and joy that filled the room. As all the people who had come there to be helped had been healed, what could Father Di Orio do but praise the Lord for the next hour and a half.

A man came up to him and gave this testimony. He had come there to disrupt the Service, to expose Father Di Orio *and* the Catholic Faith. He had been away from the Church and the Sacraments for 25 years. But, he said, when the Blessed Sacrament was raised and the Bishop blessed him, he felt something like a bolt of lightning shoot out of the monstrance and knock him down. He went on, *crying*, that he was suddenly filled with the desire to come back home to his Church.

Maybe when this man set out, he *thought* his intention was to disrupt the Service and discredit the Church; but did his Guardian Angel know his heart's true desire? Did he know that, as with the Crucifixion, what may begin as a negative can be resurrected into a positive?

Don't be afraid to send forth your Guardian Angel.

I used to worry when I would send my Guardian Angel to help a loved one, that I would be alone and unguarded. Our Church teaches that our Guardian Angel leaves and returns in a instant, moving faster than light.

When we give talks, we always ask the audience, "*How would you feel, if you discovered you were the son or daughter of the Queen of England?*" As they begin to smile and giggle a little, we continue, "*You are the child of One greater than any queen or earthly king. God, King of the Universe is your Father."* God sends down His specially created messengers and Heavenly Army to help us on our way. *How loved we are! How special we are! How royal we are!* We have personal escorts, better than those of royalty. Ours will never betray us; they can not be bought off. We have power! We have strength! There is no limit to what we can do with the help of our Angel. We need never fear again. We are not alone!

As we travel around our beautiful country and visit our Church in the different states, all we hear is, *"Why have I never heard of the Miracles of the Eucharist before this?"* And I know, the next question we will hear is why are we not hearing of the Angels and their role in our life; *why are we not being taught about the Angels?* I don't know the answer. But I do know, if ever there was a time we needed to learn and to follow the directives of the Angels, that time is now! There have never been more serious threats to our world and mankind, as a whole, than there are today.

Those who have sold out to the fallen angels would have us believe we are hopeless and helpless. They tell us there is no devil. They feed us a lot of psychological jargon, we don't understand, about this neurosis or that disfunction. They tell us there is no such thing as sin. If we speak about the Angels, they would have us believe we are simple and not up to date. Well, if their philosophy, or theology, is up to date, let us remain archaic.

Why would some have you believe that there are no Angels? If there are no Angels of God, then there are no fallen angels, and no devil, and no sin; then it follows if there is no devil and no sin why was Jesus born? The latest heresy, which is not really new at all but as old as Genesis and the fall of Adam and Eve, would have us believe that we not only don't need Angels, but we don't need God Himself as *we* are gods. Does that sound like the number one fallen angel or what?

The Guardian Angels - Teaching of the Church

Our Lord Jesus referred to the Guardian Angels when He said, "*See that you despise not one of these little ones, for I say to you that their Angels in Heaven always see the Face of My Father Who is in Heaven[6].*" He said *their* Angels, not the Angels, therefore we know that He was speaking of the Guardian Angels of the "*little ones.*" This Truth of the Guardian Angels comes to us as a revelation from the Lord, Himself. The doctrine of the Guardian Angels comes down to us, by the teaching authority of the Universal Church. It reflects Holy Scripture and our Catholic Tradition down through the ages, right from the times of the early Fathers of the Church.

St. Basil the Great said, "*...each one of the faithful has an Angel who directs his life as a teacher and a shepherd.*"

Our Saint John Chrysostom, who wrote extensively on the Angels and the Sacrifice of the Mass, said, referring to Jacob of the Old Testament, "*Every faithful Christian has an Angel, for every just man had an Angel from the very beginning.*" And then quoting Jacob: "*The Angel that nourishes me and delivers me from youth.*"

The early Fathers of the Church taught that every good Christian has the special protection of a Guardian Angel. But that is not to say that God, in His unlimited love and generous Heart, does not have the same concern and does not *likewise* grant the same fatherly protection over non-believers and sinners. They are His children, just as we are, and as their Creator, He has never stopped loving them. I believe that we, in the narrow scope of our ability to love and forgive, have a difficult time understanding how much God loves us, how He remains faithful as we turn our backs

---

[6]Mt 18:10

on Him, how He continues to love us even as we continue to take part, in His Crucifixion by crucifying others.

When I think how difficult it is to see our loved-ones go off, whether to college, to Seminary, to a Convent, to get married, or to the missions, all good things, my heart aches for our Heavenly Father Who sends His precious creations, the Angels down to be with us. How very much He loves us! And if God is willing to part with them, out of love for us, then it must be important that they are here, and it follows, we should listen to them and love them.

So now you know. There are no more excuses. When you find yourself in the occasion of sin, when the temptation is so strong to do whatever it is you know you shouldn't be doing, and an even more powerful voice within you keeps telling you not to do it, that's your Guardian Angel. Or if you are with your friends, and an instance arises where you're called upon to do something good but not necessarily popular, for someone in need but not particularly socially acceptable, when that voice inside of you urges you to go beyond yourself, pleading with you to allow yourself to be ridiculed for the sake of a child of the kingdom, that's your Guardian Angel bugging you until you give in. He won't force you, but he won't let you live either, until you do what's good for you. It's a fact that he loves you. And you can't even see him. Or can you?

PROMISE TO THE GUARDIAN ANGEL
Kneeling before Your Majesty, we thank You, O God
that You have given each of us a Heavenly companion
to be at our side, one who leads us according to Your Will
directs us to Your Glory, and manifests to us Your Love.
Here before Your eyes, we promise to love our holy companion
as a brother, and heed him when he speaks to us in the voice of
conscience. He shall surely lead us to Heaven.
LORD JESUS CHRIST, OUR SAVIOR
Take my hand and place it in the hand of my Angel, and make the sign
of Redemption over it, Your blessing for our Salvation

"On 24 December of 1922, Lucia wanted to spend the vigil of Christmas close to Padre Pio. That evening was cold and the friars had brought a brazier into the sacristy. Next to the brazier with the other women, Lucia awaited midnight to assist at the Mass that Padre Pio was to celebrate.
The three women began to doze off, while Lucia continued to recite the Rosary.
Padre Pio came down the stairway of the sacristy and stopped near the window. All of a sudden in a halo of light there appeared the Child Jesus, Who rested in Padre Pio's arms. When Padre Pio became aware that Lucia had seen the vision, he admonished her to tell no one."

St. Michael the Archangel
*His name means "Who is like God?" his battle cry
as he fought the battle against Lucifer*

Lucifer's army of fallen angels

We read, in Scripture, that the Angels were already created when God formed the Universe. *"In the dawn of that day the stars sang together, and the heavenly beings shouted for joy."*[1]

When God created the Angels, He created them with *free will*! He gave them an opportunity to choose *for* Him or *against* Him. And that choice was instant and irrevocable. Does that sound harsh? We are sure, that with all the gifts God gave to the Angels, He allowed them to see the total picture at that time: what their obedience meant to Him and what their disobedience *would* mean. The decision by Michael and the Good Angels to follow the Lord, was instant and forever, for all time in memoriam. For the fallen angels, their *disobedience* was the same.

Why would angels go against God? Why do *we* choose false gods, at times, over the One True God, Who we know will never betray us? It is said, that if you were to go to hell and invite the fallen to come out, they would refuse. Sounds crazy, doesn't it? Who would choose suffering over joy? I remember a priest saying, we go to that god we knew and worshiped, on earth. If the center of our lives is a house, or a car, or money, he said, then *that* is the god we will know when we die. *Lucifer* was the fallen angels' choice, the anti-god they chose to worship and now they know no other.

Hell is the absence of God. If you have ever lost a loved one, either to death or separation (like a divorce), and did not believe in God and hope in the Resurrection, you know what hell must be like. But it is even worse because although there is pain in memories, you at least have that *gift*. With the fallen angels, and those who are condemned to

---

[1]Job 38:7

hell, there is no gift of God, nothing but endless pain and torture. And why would anyone choose this and refuse to come out? Why would anyone choose to live in a stupor of alcoholism and drugs? Why would anyone risk everything on earth and in Heaven itself to cheat on his (or her) spouse, destroying himself and ultimately his family?

As we see the moving picture of our life, in retrospect, it becomes simpler to choose God. We can see the evidence of His Love and Peace in our life. We can look back on the world and its lies, and see more of a complete picture. Whereas with us, more and more is revealed as we *mature* in understanding, when God put the Angels to the test He allowed them to see Truth and deceit at that very moment of decision. The Angels were granted full understanding. God offered Himself and the Truth Which would never betray them. And the fallen angels chose Lucifer the *great* liar and his lies, which would always betray. Maybe, because of this there is no forgiveness for the fallen angels, as there is for us, right up to the last breath of our life.

Whatever they chose, there was no turning back. "*He commanded, and they were created; by His command they were fixed in their places forever, and they cannot disobey.*[2]" In their *pride*, they had chosen to be instruments of pain and confusion, sin and destruction. In their *poverty*, no longer in the presence of God, they would separate all God's children from Him and His unconditional Love for them, whenever they could.

Scripture says: "*He who commits sin is the slave of sin.*" The fallen angels chose the sin of pride, and they not only became the slaves of pride, but of all the other sins which quickly accompany that (pride) which is the greatest of the seven deadly sins.

---

[2]Psalm 148:6

When Lucifer fell it was through *pride*. He couldn't stand it that God would choose, through Jesus, to become *Man*. *Man who is below the angels! He would not bow down before Him! And God chose to be born of a woman! Intolerable! Another human, who was beneath him!* He would not allow *her* to be *his* queen, and so he refused to obey God, and not satisfied to disobey, alone, he led weaker angels to follow him. I can just hear Lucifer's arguments; can't you? *"What a slap in the face to us. Did He not make us, specially? Are we not the closest to Him? He betrayed us!"* This is *probably* the first time Lucifer calls God imperfect. When he turned away from God, all the evil that was possible, took over, and he called God by the names, *he*, Lucifer, would live by: Betrayer, Liar.

In the garden of Eden, when he seduced Eve it was with a *lie*. He, the author of lies dared to call the Author of Truth, a Liar. When Eve said that God told them not to eat from the tree, that they would die, he answered: *"You certainly will not die! No. God knows well that the moment you eat of it your eyes will opened and you will be like gods who know what is good and what is bad."*

Eve saw that the fruit looked good to eat - thinking of the moment and satisfying that moment only - forgetting the kindness and generosity of God the Father, she ate it. Very much like the philosophy of today. *"You deserve it! You only go around once! You have a right to happiness! It's expensive, but I'm worth it!"*

Lucifer promised her they would know as much as God, be like gods themselves. Sounds familiar, doesn't it? There is an ancient deadly heresy that has risen from hell and is spreading like a putrid disease throughout the world. It teaches that we are gods! We are told we do not need God; that we are gods, the masters of our own fate. And what happens when, like Adam and Eve, we eat of *that* fruit and our eyes are opened to our nakedness, our weakness, the soft clay we are made of? What happens when what is revealed to us is that we are nothing outside of our Creator? Do we believe Lucifer's lies that God will never forgive us, and despair? I don't think so. Our Guardian Angel, who we may have put aside, the way you do those who tell you what you are about to do will harm you, is there waiting to lead us home to the Arms of our Father in Heaven.

And so, the war began with Adam and Eve. Because of one act of pride and disobedience, the world would suffer until the Second Coming of Christ. Why wouldn't they listen to Christ when he came, the first time? Why do we continue to kill one another, lie to one another, speak out against one another, refuse to love one another as Jesus commanded us? Because the old battle goes on, and the general in charge of that army of dissidents (the fallen angels), Lucifer, is still spreading his lies. And we, children of Adam and Eve, instead of listening to our *new* Adam and Eve, our Lord Jesus and His Mother Mary, are listening to the *evil one*, and suffering.

God does not punish us so much as we punish ourselves. God, our most perfect and loving Father made rules because, knowing Parent that he is, He knows what will make us happy. And how do we know when it is God? Listen to our Guardian Angel. He is with us to guide us, to protect us, to light the way to, *yes*, our Lord. God has sent him as a messenger to bring His Word to us. We don't dare *not* listen!

The scorned one.

They say, there is no fury like a woman scorned. Well, maybe that is a gift left to us by our first mother Eve, given to her by Lucifer. Because I believe when Lucifer turned away from God and suffered the total absence of God, he felt that rejection so completely, he knew a fury so volatile, it set part of the Universe on fire and we have hell.

After his attack on Adam and Eve, God punished Lucifer, banning him from all animals and wild creatures, condemning him to crawl on his belly, eating dirt the rest of his life. Lucifer became furious, not repentant. He set about, right from the beginning to try to hurt God. And how, *best*, could he hurt God? Hurt His children, His creation molded from the depths of His Heart.

Adam and Eve had two children: Cain and Abel. Cain, their first born tilled the soil and his brother Abel tended the flocks. Each brought an offering to the Lord. God was pleased with the gift of Abel, "*one of the best firstlings of his flock.*" Abel did not bring the Lord just any offering, but the very best. He trusted that the Lord would provide for him out of *His* Bounty. He showed the Lord that he trusted in Him, that He was the God of his life.

Now, "*Cain brought an offering to the Lord from the fruit of the soil.*" God was pleased with Abel's offering, but looked down upon Cain's. Abel gave from his substance. Had Cain given from his excess? Cain was upset and resentful because God favored Abel's gift over his. Again, the Lord, Faithful and Patient Parent, reached out. He told Cain not to be downhearted, but to try again. He told him if he did well, he could hold up his head. Did God recognize that possibly this gift of Cain's was given out of pride and not love? Did he do it for the praise and recognition he would receive, rather than out of love freely given?

The Lord warned Cain: "*If you do well, you can hold up your head; but if not, sin is a demon lurking at your door; his urge is toward you, yet you can be his master.*" Was God saying: Repent, my child. Do not envy your brother. Do not covet *his* gift, but bring me a gift of your *heart*, your love. Bring me your treasure. I will not be outdone in generosity. But, if you do not make Me the priority, the focus, the Master of your life, there is another waiting (a demon).

Scripture uses the word *"lurking"*. The devil wants you to suffer with him, the unquenchable fires of Hell.

God warns Cain, the devil will not let up on him. But, God consoles: *"You can be his master."* Teresa of Avila said that more powerful than any evil spirit, is the man who allows the demon to work through him, the one who says *yes* to him. The fallen angels can do nothing without our consent. Is that not what God was saying to Cain? Is that not what God is saying to us? You are not helpless and hopeless. You are not slaves. You have free will. *Use it to love Me*, says the Lord. *Use it to know that Peace that only I, the Lord can give you.*

The Battle Goes on!

We come to the modern world where the Bible itself is often disputed, where men have the audacity to question whether Jesus actually spoke the words attributed to Him in the Gospel, passed down over the centuries by the Catholic Church; why, then, are we so shocked and surprised that the authenticity of the Angels is also under attack; because to attack the *reality* of the Angels is to invalidate half the pages of the Old and New Testaments. We have to come to terms with the fact that the battle of the Angels has never really ended. To quote St. Paul, *"For our wrestling is not against flesh and blood, but against the Principalities and the Powers.*[3]*"*

"I believe in man!"

It was around the year 1978. We were at a Bible study. I opened the door to a young man, who was with two other young people who regularly attended the Bible study. When I looked at him, my first reaction was fear. I didn't want to let him in. I was shocked by his appearance. He was dirty; his hair was long; he was wearing bikers' boots. But then I

---

[3]Eph 6:11-12

thought, there I was being prejudiced against him because he reminded me of that terrible time, the sixties and drugs.

I invited him into the kitchen to have some refreshment. When the little dog, Tuffy, saw him, he began to snarl. His hair stood up on end. No amount of pleading would make him stop. We had never seen him like that. I apologized to the young man for Tuffy's unusual behavior, explaining he considered himself a little watch-dog. He came back with, *"Oh, I hate dogs and they hate me. My father loves dogs and hates me and I hate him."* His voice was like a machine gun spitting out the words. I thought *hate*? He is speaking hate, hate, hate. Isn't Bible Study a place where we learn of love and the Lover through His Word? What was he doing here? But then, I thought, there I go again. The young man was probably a victim of the propaganda being fed to our young people of *"generation gap"* and *let's hate our parents or we cannot grow up* - a way of breaking away from family ties and on to adulthood.

I noticed he didn't have a Bible. I offered him one. He refused; he wouldn't even touch it. A chill went through my body. Again, I thought this strange. But judging *there I go again*, I let it go. The group began to pray. I mentioned how devious the *evil one* was, how *underhanded* he was. A young girl started to share how, in her life, the devil would subtly work on her head and soul until recognizing him, she rebuked him.

The young man burst out, again sputtering hate, in an almost robot-like manner: *"There is no devil."* My husband challenged; *"If you don't believe in the devil, do you believe in God?"* I was kind of shocked when Bob said that. That sounded kind of rude. Why did he say that! Before I could try to sooth things over, the young man burst out: *"I believe in man!"*

When we left the Bible Study, I told Bob I was worried. I knew all the young man had to do was pretend he was confused about God and the Faith, and he would be able to remain, after everyone left. Like most husbands, Bob always would accuse me of needless worry; but this time it was different. He agreed, we needed to call the leader of the bible study as soon as we returned home. She told us that not only did she know *who* he was, but several of the people, as they left, warned her. She also shared, as he was leaving, the young man said she would see him the next week. She replied, "*No, we know who you are, and you are not welcome here.*"

"*I believe in man.*" It sounded all too familiar. *Who* believes in man? Isn't that the teaching of the devil? *Bow down before me and I will give you the world.* Isn't that what the cults are teaching, today? This guru and that channeler. You are the master of your own fate. A woman takes the precious name of our Madonna and commits all kinds of abominations against God, even to the point of using a Rosary as part of her sick act. How did that start? She has a good singing voice. Did the evil one tell her she needed a gimmick, and what better one than to blaspheme against the Mother of God and God Himself?

Theologians when going for a Doctorate need to have a paper published. They are told no one will publish it if it isn't *different*, controversial; and so, very often they come up with all kinds of conjectures and new theories. Then, so they can sleep at night, they begin to believe these hypotheses, or theories, themselves.

Also, there are those who, *knowing* the Truth they were taught, are fooled into believing they can give a professor, who is teaching heresy, what he wants, in order to get a passing grade, but still be able to hold onto what they really believe - the Truths of the Roman Catholic Church. What happens when they wake up and the pretenses have become their realities? What happens when, as with our first mother Eve, the knowledge they sought and the promises that were made are all lies? Now, believing in *man*, they feel betrayed and are devastated because they believe they cannot change and go back. Of course they can, with the God Who is always waiting with open Arms, this God they traded in for the moment. But pretending for so long He didn't exist, they judge they cannot turn to Him, and fall into despair. The apple that tasted so delicious is now sour!

Why would someone who doesn't believe in God go to a Bible Study? And why wasn't he successful in disrupting the evening and the work of the Lord? Because for as many fallen angels that were there trying to lead us away from God, that evening, there were that many more *Holy Angels* because of the prayers of the faithful there, praying. The fallen angels are busy, no, *busier* than they have ever been because we are in such crucial times. And in times such as these, we need the guidance and protection of the Heavenly Army of Angels, more than ever, against the enemies of Christ who are roaming the world seeking the ruination of souls. In times such as these we must pray more.

Prayer, the Priesthood and the Angels.

One night, Bob and I went to Mass, at our parish church. Although we had gone to Mass that morning, we went again. There was a special speaker that night. Members of our parish had gone to lectures and attended Mass with the priest celebrating the Mass, and they said he was truly filled with the Holy Spirit.

The Mass began with the most beautiful and reverent reading of the opening prayers. When the priest read the Gospel, it came to life. His homily was inspiring. I felt tears coming to my eyes. I looked over at Bob. He was touched, too. Something happened. I still can't explain it. One moment he was preaching about the Gospel and the next he was attacking the Angels! It was as if a serpent had slithered up his body and bit his tongue.

At first, I thought I had heard incorrectly or misunderstood what he was saying. When Bob asked rather definitely, *"Are you ready to go?"*, I knew I was not the only one. I protested, *"Give him a chance. Let's see where he is going with this."* I just knew he was going to turn it around, and make it positive some way. Maybe he was playing devil's *advocate* and trying to arouse strong feelings in us for the Angels by attacking them. Oh, I said and thought everything, just so I could keep my illusions of the priest.

Then, he turned on Mother Mary. By the time we left the church, he was saying he did not know why people found it so peculiar, he was traveling with a woman companion. The next day, I went to confession. I told our parish priest I was truly sorry I had left the church before the end of the Mass. (It was the first and only time I have ever done that.) He said *he* had left shortly after we did.

The priest who had suddenly turned against the Angels and their Queen Mary, we found out later, left the church and married his traveling companion. He is now a key note speaker at non-Catholic meetings, speaking out against the Church's teaching on Mother Mary, calling her no more a virgin than he was, and ridiculing our belief in the Angels, which dates back to the Old Testament.

We know that when we sing the Holy Holy Holy, we are accompanying the Angels as they sing to the Lord on High. When the priest calls down the Holy Spirit at the beginning of the Eucharistic prayer, we know thousands of Angels accompany Him, descending upon the Altar of Sacrifice. How can a priest, who is in the presence of the Lord *alive* in the Eucharist, who is surrounded by the Holy Angels, turn against all he had professed to believe in, on the day of his ordination?

There are so many evil, fallen angels. When Jesus died, He took the worst negative, His death on the Cross, and turned it into the greatest positive, our Redemption.

When the fallen angels, led by Lucifer, turned away from God, they took the greatest positive, God's Gifts to them, and turned them into the worst of negatives, the leading of His children away from Him to eternal damnation. And what better way to go about doing this, than to tempt those the Lord has chosen, His pastors. I wonder, if there had been enough people at Mass, aware what was happening, and if we all had prayed to our Guardian Angels, if maybe the fallen angels would have been defeated and we would still have a holy priest in our Church.

Before you judge that priest, remember parishioners had said, how filled he had been with the Holy Spirit. One of the holiest people we have ever interviewed once said, "*I pray for the Grace to believe, every day.*" Had the priest stopped praying for that Grace? Did the fallen angels tell him that was just one of the myths Sister Mary Regina had taught him in Grammar School?

When the fallen angel of pride comes in

One day, at our daily Mass, we heard a priest say, how disillusioned he was when he learned upon entering the Seminary, that everything the good Sisters had taught him were all lies. This young priest, who talked down about most of our traditions, always injecting new hypotheses about who said what, and what really happened (it didn't matter if it was in agreement with the Word or the Church's teaching), looked *sad* as he said those words. When the fallen angel of Pride told him he was too intelligent, too learned to believe in the Angels, was that when he was robbed of all his beliefs? A priest once said that when you let the fallen angel of *Pride* in, the door swings wide open and all the other fallen angels, with their poison, come rushing in.

A priest comes back

Then there was the young priest who had been associate pastor at a parish where our family had once belonged. Years later, when we returned to our parish for the fortieth anniversary of our former pastor, the young priest who had been very close to our son, came over to speak to us. He told us how he had left the Priesthood and the Church for five years. He shared that one day, he knocked on the door of the Cardinal's Rectory and asked if he could come back. The Cardinal replied, "*I don't want to know where you have been or what you have done. I just want to welcome you back.*" Could it have been his Guardian Angel who had given him the idea to go home to his Father, much like the prodigal son of the Gospel?

Why does one priest leave and one return? I think it is matter of prayer. When we pray, we call upon the Angels and they do the rest. Why not try it?

"I rebuke you in the Name of Jesus Christ!"

You have heard it said, there are no fallen angels and the devil does not exist. I would like to share a true story of a young man we met at our parish church, some years ago. We fell in love with him and his family. They were a beautiful sign in the church. You could see how much they loved one another and the Lord. We would see them at Mass, every Sunday. He attended Legion of Mary meetings. He and his wife went on a Marriage Encounter weekend. Whenever you saw him, he had a Bible under his arm.

We began to invite him and his family over to the house after Mass or after some of the meetings at church. One Saturday, he and his wife were at our home helping price gifts for the Octoberfest, a fund and fun raising get-together the church had once a year, to help finance our school.

I went into the kitchen. I heard the young man confiding to Bob, "*I was an alcoholic for twelve years.*" I held my breath. This gentle, loving, holy young man, an alcoholic? He went on,

"I went to work every day; My boss considered me one of his best and most dependable workers. At night, I would come home, sometimes not even eat and begin to drink until I passed out on the couch. I was never physically or mentally abusive to my wife and children. But, now I know I was hurting them; because, by withholding love, giving it to another love, my alcohol, I was depriving them of life-giving love. One night, I fell into my usual stupor on the couch. It seemed this night would be like all the other 365 nights in each of the twelve years of my drinking, with me sleeping it off, awakening the next morning, going into work, with no one the wiser.

"But tonight was to be different. I shot up from the couch. There was someone there! As I focused my eyes, before me was a creature, not man not beast. He was hideous! I trembled, as I asked him who he was. He introduced himself, 'I am the devil of drugs!' As he described all his powers, bragging he was the mightiest and the deadliest of the fallen angels, he became more and more grotesque. 'I break up marriages. I kill. I cause men and women to cheat and steal. I am responsible for most infidelity. Suicide is a specialty of mine. Age is no barrier against my advances. When I take over in a life, there is no love a person would not give up for me."

The young man was crying, as he went on, seeing in his life, how completely he had turned away from all he held dear for this false mistress. He told Bob, he cried out, with all the strength, he could muster, *"I rebuke you in the Name of Jesus Christ!"* And the fallen angel of drugs and destruction, disappeared. He shared that not only had he not had a drink from that day to this, almost ten years later, but he has never *desired* a drink.

Are we defenseless? Are we alone? Do we cry out, with Saints Paul and Augustine: *"What happens is that I do, not the good I will to do, but the evil I do not intend...This means that even though I want to do what is right, a law that leads to wrongdoing is always at hand..."* And then when we

feel like we are going down for the last count, we feel a surge
of energy and we are up and fighting the good fight, running
the race and finishing it and all for the Glory of God.

I'm not finished yet, Lord.

We were in a plane, flying to Birmingham, Alabama, on
our way to Eternal Word Television Network to tape a
television series, based on our book **Saints and other
Powerful Men in the Church.** The pilot had announced we
would be landing early, and here it was fifteen minutes after
our scheduled arrival time, and we could not see the airport,
no less the landing strip. The captain's voice came over loud
and clear, *"We apologize for the delay. It looks as if we cannot
land for another hour and a half; we are in the midst of a really
bad storm, and the visibility is too poor."* The ride became
really rough, as we circled the airport. Our plane was not
able to climb; we could see the other planes circling over us.
Suddenly we were in a blanket of clouds. It was as if we
were being swallowed up by huge puffs of smoke from an
unseen giant. We began to pray! Somehow, instead of
petitioning the Lord to save us, we found what was coming
out were words of praise and thanksgiving.

*"Thank you, Lord for the family You have given us.
Thank You, Lord for choosing us for one another. Thank you,
Lord for the Love You have shown us. Thank You Lord for
our Community."* We found ourselves, for almost half an
hour, praising Him for all the wondrous gifts our Lord had
bestowed upon us, when we came to, *"Praise You, Lord for
the gift of the Apostolate You have given us."* And then we
realized..."*Lord we cannot die. We have not finished the book
on the Angels."* The Angels! That's it! They could not allow
the plane to go down. They wanted the faithful to know
about how they were there, and have always been there to
help.

Just as we finished praying those last words of praise, the sky opened up. We were now flying in the bluest of skies. It was as if the clouds had been swept away. *The Angels?*

"Are you the priest who had everyone on the Plane praying?"

Father Harold Cohen shared, one day when the plane, he was in, was experiencing turbulence, he started to pray *silently* to the Guardian Angels of everyone in the plane to join in with his Guardian Angel and pray for their safe landing. As he looked out the window, he saw what appeared to be hundreds of Angels encircling the plane.

The plane landed safely and smoothly. As Father Cohen was walking away from the plane, he overheard one of the passengers sharing, *"There's the priest who had everyone on the plane praying."*

†

And so, the battle goes on and the war is not yet won. The battle lines are drawn. At the forefront of God's Army of Holy Angels is the Queen of Angels, Mary Most Holy. Her mantle is flying, covering those faithful who are bringing up the rear. Right behind Mother Mary are legions of Angels. Following close by, their Guardian Angels leading the way, are the rest of God's Warriors, the faithful, the dry and wet martyrs who each day say yes to the Lord and *no* to His enemies who would lead them away from Him.

They are a brilliant and powerful force as they march forward to do battle. They are not many, at first, but as they walk on, more and more join them, at first, out of curiosity. *What would make someone give up his life, for Someone he cannot see?* After they walk a while, they begin to hear the praises of the Angels mingled with those of the faithful in the rear. Suddenly they recognize *their* voices. They are singing! They are praising God! They are praying to God Most High! They have never been so happy. And before they know it, they are no longer tagging along but are part of God's Army.

Opposite, advancing toward them, are the enemy forces. In front, is Lucifer himself. This once most beautiful angel is now *ugly*. All the sins, and the blood he has caused to be shed, have erupted into open sores on his face and body. His once beautiful body is now twisted and gnarled. There is not a hint of the once magnificent angel so loved by the Lord. His eyes are cold and unseeing. His mouth is twisting with rage. But wait, I see something else. Is it fear?

Cowering behind Lucifer, are the fallen angels who followed him away from God's Grace. The haughtiness and confidence they portrayed as they performed their dirty work on earth, has been replaced by almost a stealthiness. Like their leader, they are not too sure of their back-up. It seems the platoon bringing up the rear is thinning out.

With each dawn, instead of new-comers, they are experiencing defections. No amount of promises or rosy pictures will keep them in the ranks.

Could it be, that the Guardian Angels of those in the rear of Lucifer's army have never stopped reaching out to their individual charges, pointing, over and over again, to the road leading to the Lord and Peace? And could it be, because of this faithful dedication to the Truth, by the Holy Angels, this mass exodus is coming about? I don't know; what do you think?

We know that good is stronger than evil. We know that Jesus and His band of glorious Angels will triumph in the end. That's never been in doubt. The question is, *Will we be with them? Will we be one of those saints who go marching in? The decision is ours.*

Left:
Jesus and the Angel in the Garden of Gethsemane

Below:
Mosaic on Altar on Mount Tabor

The Birth of Jesus

Jesus and the Angels

To say that the Angels' greatest roles on earth were on behalf of our Savior, Our Lord Jesus Christ, is an understatement. As we track the life of Our Lord, we see just a little of how intricate a role they played, from the Annunciation to the Ascension. When we follow in the footsteps of Jesus, we begin to understand the importance of the Angels in our own journey. We want to share with you the highlights of how the Angels protected and ministered to the Savior here on earth.

The Archangel Gabriel has always been considered the Angel of the Incarnation, the Miracle of God becoming Man. We really believe it goes even farther than that. Gabriel was the leader of the Angels who ministered to Jesus all His life, from the Annunciation to the Ascension. We speak about Gabriel's role in the Annunciation to Mary, in a different chapter. Here, we want to focus on the intricate role of the Angels in the drama of the life of Jesus.

St. Joseph and the Angels

Joseph is a key figure in the early life of Jesus, and also the motivating force the Angels used to carry out the movements of the Holy Family. After Gabriel left Mary on that momentous day of the Annunciation, when he told her she would be the Mother of God, her thoughts went to Joseph. She loved him dearly. There was a bond between them that was so strong. He had always trusted her completely. When she met with him, and explained the events of the Annunciation to him, she scrutinized his eyes. He was sad; he was hurt; he didn't believe her. He didn't trust her. Joseph was going to divorce Mary quietly. Nothing *she* said could convince him that she was telling the truth. There's a good chance St. Anne, Mary's mother, came to her aid. Still, he couldn't accept it. It's understandable.

Would you believe such a story if your teenage girl told you that's how she got pregnant? Would anyone believe it? It took an *Angel's intercession* to finally make Joseph believe that Mary was telling the truth.

An Angel came to Joseph in a dream, and confirmed Mary's story to him. He told Joseph it was all right to take her as his wife. We know that Joseph was relieved. He loved Mary. How could he help but love her. But it took the Angels to persuade him. As we see the Angels working in the life of Our dear Savior, we have confidence that they have been given to us to help us, too.

One of the most outstanding examples of the Angelic presence in the life of Jesus came at the Birth of the Lord. First, we're given the gift of the Angel Gabriel, appearing to the shepherds in the field, trying to calm their fears, and at the same time give them the Good News that the King of the Jews had been born. Once their fears were allayed, *"Suddenly, a great Army of Heaven's Angels appeared..."*[1] The sky was filled with the brilliance of the Angels. Night turned into day. The Glory of God manifested Itself on the shepherds through the Angels.

But what effect did they have on Joseph? The gentle sound of the newborn Baby crying, woke Joseph. He looked around the cave, aware for the first time of the brilliance of the light shining in. The first thing he saw was Mary's face. It was illuminated. She held the softest, whitest, most delicate child, Joseph had ever seen. The King, the Messiah, was born! *The Word was made Flesh!*

At first, Joseph didn't know what to do. How do you behave in the presence of God? He was awkward. But the gentle Mary, who had changed from girl into wise woman in nine short months, motioned him with her eyes. He would be responsible for this Child's welfare for many years. It was

---

[1]Lk 2:13

time to get used to it. They arranged Him comfortably in a bed of hay. Mary lay next to Him, with Joseph kneeling at her side. The light dimmed. The Angels went into a protection mode, stationing themselves all around the cave, keeping those *out* who should not enter, and allowing those *in* whom the Lord wanted in.

Joseph and Mary were exhausted from the excitement of the evening. Their eyes grew heavy. They began to doze, when they heard the shuffling of feet outside the cave. Joseph jumped to his feet; he saw simple shepherds entering the cave. They told Joseph that they had seen Angels in the fields, singing praises to God for the birth of the Savior. The Angels told the shepherds to come to this cave in Bethlehem, where they would see the King of the World. They looked at the Baby nestled in Mary's arms. They knelt and paid homage to Him. Joseph was speechless; he couldn't believe the scene he was watching, the words he was hearing. But he would learn to trust the Lord, and accept His gifts and help, as given him by the Angels over his lifetime.

The Angels had a marked influence on St. Joseph. Three times in Scripture, they came to him, always in a dream. They gave him instruction, and he obeyed like a shot, without question or hesitation. Remember Zechariah? He questioned the Angel Gabriel regarding the birth of John the Baptist, and was struck dumb. Joseph, on the other hand, being given news and instruction of much greater importance, which would have more of a radical effect on his life and that of his family's, never questioned, never doubted.

The Angel appeared to Joseph in a dream a second time. He told him to take Jesus and His Mother Mary, and flee. *"Herod will be looking for the Child in order to kill Him.*

*So get up, take the Child and His Mother and escape to Egypt,
and stay there until I tell you to leave."*[2]

Now, you want to talk about *obedience?* In the very
next passage, Scripture tells us *"Joseph got up, took the Child
and His Mother, and left during the night for Egypt."* He didn't
wait until morning; he didn't stock up on provisions; he *left!*
He went to a foreign land, where Jews may not have been
too welcome. What would you do if you had a dream where
an Angel told you to get up, take your family to the airport,
board a plane for Iraq or Iran, and stay there until further
notice? Would you do it? Would you speculate on it first?
Might you not have a family meeting, and measure the pros
and cons of it? Would you wait until the first rays of
sunlight, have a few cups of coffee, and hopefully make a
more rational decision? *"He left during the night for Egypt."*
The Lord has given the Angels such power!

A very interesting and important bond developed
between Joseph and the Angel in Matthew's Gospel. The
Angel said to Joseph, "...stay there until *I* tell you to leave."
We get from that, an ongoing relationship between the same
Angel and Joseph. This leads us to believe, the Angel
(Gabriel?) and most likely, many others, would be there, on
call, twenty four hours a day, *as long as the Savior was on the
earth!* Perhaps that's what gave Joseph the confidence to
make such a radical move immediately upon receiving the
order from the Angel. Maybe that's what gave Joan of Arc
the confidence to listen to the words of her Angels, and obey
them. Possibly, the Angels have been trying to tell us to have
faith that the instruction they give us every moment of every
day, which we sometimes call the voice of our consciences, is
for us to act on, *now!*

A period of time passed. We don't know how long the
Holy Family stayed in Egypt. It was most likely for a number

---

[2]Mt 2:13

of years, until Herod died. Once again, an Angel came to St. Joseph in a dream. *"Get up, take the Child and His Mother, and go back to the land of Israel, because those who tried to kill the Child are dead."* Joseph obeyed. The Angel gave him instructions to return to Nazareth, which he followed.

Scripture is silent about the life of Jesus from twelve to thirty. This gives rise to a great deal of speculation as to the activity of the Angels during that time. We can only base our assumptions on how they worked in His life before and after those years. They were always there, helping Him, not letting the young Jesus trip on a rock and fall, not letting danger of any kind affect Him or His Family.

There is also nothing in Scripture regarding the death of St. Joseph, but after parenting Jesus, teaching Him, caring for Him, protecting Him, loving Him, traveling with Him throughout his early life; and recalling St. Joseph's devotion and obedience to the Angels, our minds and hearts soar upward to another place and another time and we see a huge welcoming committee waiting for Joseph, in Paradise. As St. Joseph gave up his spirit to the Father he always loved, we are sure his eyes travelled from Mary to Jesus. He could feel the beat of Jesus' Heart as He held him close. He didn't want to leave his two most precious loved ones on earth, but as he forced his eyes and heart from them, he looked ahead to his eternal life with the Father and with Them some day. As the *last* image his mortal eyes beheld were Jesus and Mary, most likely, the *first* image his glorified eyes gazed upon were the joyful Angels, thousands and tens of thousands of Angels, welcoming this man of hope, home.

There's a scripture passage, Hebrews 11:1-2, which tells us *"Faith is confident assurance concerning what we hope for, and convictions about things we cannot see."* We believe that describes Joseph very well. He listened to the words of the Angels, and obeyed them. He was told about Jesus, Who He was, and what His mission was to be. Scripture doesn't ever give us an indication that he saw any of these promises fulfilled. Again, this is all open to the Holy Spirit whispering in our ears. What did Joseph experience from His foster-Son Jesus? Did Jesus give St. Joseph insights which were never recorded in the Gospel? Did St. Joseph receive a vision of Heaven, of the fulfillment of the promises he did not see on earth, or did he live his life on pure faith? We'll never know the answers to these questions until our own personal Angel brings us on a tour of the Kingdom, and then, of course, it won't matter, because we'll be there.

Jesus and the Angels

We know *feelings*! It's hard to envision anyone without feelings. There are those who will tell you Angels don't have feelings, but Jesus teaches us, "*I tell you, the Angels of God rejoice over one sinner who repents.*" When you visit the Church of the Transfiguration, way up high on Mount Tabor in the Holy Land, you discover a series of mosaics surrounding the main altar. The most touching of the mosaics for us, is the one depicting three Angels, with the Lamb of God laying at the feet of one of the Angels. The Lamb's throat is slit. Blood is pouring out. He is just laying there, dying. The Angels stand above the Lamb, surrounding Him, their eyes sad, directed Heavenward, tears streaming down their faces. As you, too, feel and taste salty tears spilling from your own eyes, you know this was an inspired work, and you have no problem believing Angels have feelings!

Angels are very focused; they give glory to God in the Trinity, Father, Son and Holy Spirit. The joy of their existence is giving glory to God. They are totally committed to the Trinity. If they had bodies, we would have to say their hearts would burst from the Beatific Vision. That's why we find it so difficult to believe they could just unemotionally stand there during Jesus' temptation on the mountain, and do nothing. Jesus had stayed on that mountain for forty days and nights, without food, trying to empty Himself of all human weakness, to strengthen Himself for the job ahead. But His humanity clicked in; He became very hungry.

When Satan realized this, He attacked in the only way he knew, sneaky. He was allowed to manifest himself in a form that Jesus could recognize. The Angels, on the other hand, had to stay in the background. They were there; but they had to allow the temptation to take place. Now we know that Jesus could have sent Satan packing at any time. He could have instructed His Angels to send him to the moon. But it was necessary for Our Savior to give the prince of darkness his time, and it was a strong discipline for the Angels to stand by, and not crush the little vermin with their pinky toes. Not until it was over, when Jesus made it very clear who was boss, and dismissed the devil with *"Away with you, Satan! Scripture has it, 'You shall do homage to the Lord, your God; Him alone shall you adore.'"*[3], were the Angels allowed to manifest themselves and minister to their Lord.

But do you really believe they weren't touched by what was going on during this battle? Do we think they had no feelings about what the Lord was suffering? Do we imagine they did nothing while their God was waging battle with the evil one? We doubt that very much. We contend they were using the most powerful weapon they had, doing the mightiest thing they could do, what they were created to do, *pray!* They knew and know the power of prayer. Their prayer weakened Satan and strengthened Jesus, the Man. It was their heavy-duty ammunition, and they knew just how to use it.

The Angels and the Passion of Jesus

On a similar vein, we read about the involvement of the Angels in the Garden of Gethsemane, during Jesus'

---

[3]Mt 4:10

Agony. We only become aware of their presence when the worst of it had ended, when Jesus had sweat blood, when His humanity cried out for another chance; when He suffered His greatest temptation and asked the Father to take it away. It wasn't until after He said, "*Not My will, however, but Your will be done*[4]," that sounds of another great Fiat echoed throughout the Heavens, "*Let it be done to me according to Your will.*[5]" Like Mother, like Son.

Only then, after Our Lord Jesus had gone through this part of the drama of the Triumph of the Cross, were the Angels allowed to come and minister to Him. St. Luke only writes of *one* Angel ministering to the Lord. We would have to believe it was more like *thousands* of Angels, surrounding Jesus, giving Him strength for the journey, which would take Him down through the deepest, darkest foulest-smelling valleys, *the Crucifixion*, but would ultimately carry Him to the highest Place, far above the earth, where the air was clean, and a sweet scent of Heavenly flowers permeated His nostrils, *the Resurrection*.

The Angels' job in the Garden of Gethsemane was extremely difficult. Jesus was distressed. He was being asked to let go of His last possession, His favored three, Peter, James and John. He knew how Peter would betray Him later on that evening. He had foretold it. But He had to let go of James and John as well. These were the three He had always trusted, Simon and the Sons of Thunder. He trusted them, and they betrayed Him, not because they were bad, but because they were human. They fell asleep. After each bout with His agony, He went back to them. He was hurt, as He cried out; "*Could you not stay awake one hour with Me?*" And after each appeal, they gave into the weakness of the flesh; they went back to sleep. He had to

---

[4] Lk 22:42
[5] Lk 1:38

see their shortcomings, their humanity. There were many things which may have gone through the mind of the Savior, such as, "*These are the ones whom I spent three years teaching?*" or "*This is what I'm leaving behind to continue the work I began?*", or perhaps "*Never put your trust in man; there is truly only one God.*" And through all this, He had to trust that somehow, the Father was going to make all of it right.

Then the prince of darkness made his entrance, in the form of Judas. The soldiers attacked; they took Jesus and bound His Hands. Peter's mind was reeling. It was all falling apart. This was not the way it was supposed to happen. *These men were seizing God!* It didn't make any sense. He did the only thing he knew; he drew his sword and lashed out at anyone, anywhere. He struck a servant, severing his ear. Perhaps he cried out in his mind, "*Where are the Angels to protect You and defend You?*" Did the Angels raise their swords to follow Peter's lead? But Jesus stopped him *(and perhaps the Angels as well)* with one word, "*Enough!*" Then Jesus put it all together. He turned to the chief priests, the chiefs of the temple guard, and very possibly His gaze rested on Judas. "*But this is your hour, the triumph of darkness.*"

This time, Thursday night to Friday at 3 p.m., had to have been the longest and most difficult for the Angels. Even if they were privileged to know the triumph Jesus was to experience through the Cross, the living of it was hard. Scripture doesn't give us indicators of any action on the part of the Heavenly Army during this, the most disgraceful period in the history of the world. They had to stand by and watch the dishonor being heaped on their God. This well-oiled, invincible machine of the Lord, could not do anything but stand there and watch the Passion and Death of their God being played out in front of them.

Try to visualize a great field of battle, with your troops standing on a hill, waiting to be called into action. You outnumber your enemy greatly; you are far superior in

fighting skills. Your King, your leader, goes before you onto
the field to talk peace terms with the enemy. They respond
by beating and mocking and torturing and finally killing your
King, and your troops are not allowed to lift one hand to
defend Him in any way. You can only stand there, arms and
weapons at your side, and *watch*.

This is how we envision the *Heavenly Army of Angels*
during that terrible period in our Church, when our God-
made-Man was being killed. At one point, it seemed like the
Angels might be called into battle. They listened intently, as
Jesus spoke to Pontius Pilate.

*"My kingdom does not belong to this world.   If My
kingdom were of this world, my subjects (the Angels) would be
fighting to save me from being handed over to the Jews."*[6]

Did they perk up, begin to pick up their spiritual battle
gear, flex their muscles, and prepare for the battle of their
existence? Jesus spoke again. *"As it is My kingdom is not
here."*

And so they stood there again, keeping the Death
Watch. They suffered with Jesus every blow, every whip,
every spit, every degradation, physical as well as emotional.
Jesus had already told the people who were killing Him that
He was God; they wouldn't believe Him. But the actions of
these people had to be incredulous to the Angels, who *knew*
this was God. How could anyone treat God in this way, and
such a giving, loving God?

We can envision the Angels experiencing tears and
justified anger as they watched the scandal of the Crucifixion
unfold. Mother Angelica tells us the only *justified anger* is
God's anger. There have been many instances of God's
Anger in the history of the world. We believe the six million
massacred by Hitler incurred God's Anger, and the ten
million Stalin murdered aroused God's Anger, as well as the

---

[6]Jn 18:36

twenty three million unborn babies we Americans have slaughtered, inflict God's Anger. But this, the murder of His only Son, Our God, we *truly* believe this was a time of God's anger, and He allowed the Angels to manifest it for Him.

"*My God, My God, why have You forsaken Me?*" Did they cry out to Jesus, "*No, Lord, God your Father has not forsaken you! We have not forsaken You. It is those down there with You, those you came to save, they have forsaken You, Lord, not us. We love You. Give us one word, one sign and we'll make our slaughter of the 185,000 Assyrian soldiers[7] who insulted You, seem like child's play. Give us the nod, Lord, and we'll wipe out every one of them.*"

As Jesus cried His last cry and painfully breathed His last breath, could it have been the screams of the Angels, horrified by the blasphemous act of our loving Savior's murder, that caused the curtain to be torn in the Temple from top to bottom, the earth to shake violently, the rocks to split, the sun to blacken, and the graves to open? Could that massive convulsion of the earth have been caused by the justified anger of God, as conveyed to us by His Angels?

But the scandal of the Cross became the Triumph of the Cross. As the sun sets, the sun also rises. "*By dying, You destroyed our death; by rising, You restored our life, Lord Jesus, come in Glory.*" Praise You, Lord. Thank You Lord. On the third day, God turned it all around. He changed death into life. Matthew gives us an excellent description of what happened.

"*After the Sabbath, as Sunday morning was dawning, Mary Magdalene and the other Mary went to look at the tomb. Suddenly there was a violent earthquake; an Angel of the Lord came down from Heaven, rolled the stone away, and sat on it. His appearance was like lightning, and his clothes were white as snow. The*

---

[7] 2 Kg:19:35

guards were so afraid that they trembled and became like dead men."[8]

The Angel who instilled such fear in the hearts of the Roman guards, was the same one who spoke so very gently to the women who came to the tomb. Anticipating their fears, he rolled back the stone, before they arrived. He calmed them. He gave them instructions for the Apostles. He watched them as they ran off. His instructions from the Lord had been to give the word to the women first. He knew they would get the job done. They were to be trusted. Was it Gabriel who appeared to the women? In the litany of the Holy Angels[9], Gabriel is given the title of Angel of the Incarnation, as well as Protector of all servants and handmaids of God. We bet it was Gabriel.

The Alpha and the Omega, the beginning and the end. The Angels were there for all of it. The first mention of the Angels in the life of Jesus was at the Annunciation; the last mention of the Angels in the life of Jesus was when He ascended to Heaven to summon the Holy Spirit. The Angels were there.

"They still had their eyes fixed on the sky as He (Jesus) went away, when two men dressed in white suddenly stood beside them and said, 'Galileans, why are you standing there looking up at the sky? This Jesus, who was taken from you into Heaven, will come back in the same way that you saw Him go to Heaven.'"[10]

The Apostles left the hill in Bethany, and made their way back to the Upper Room in Jerusalem. They were confused; their Master had left. His words about the Holy Spirit coming, didn't sink in yet. They didn't understand. However, they went on their way, to begin the Church as we know it today. The Angels watched the followers of Jesus

---

[8]Mt 28:1-5
[9]Opus Angelorum, Fatima
[10]Acts 1:10-11

leave. They understood the words of Jesus. They knew what was going to happen on Pentecost Sunday. These dear men would be so filled with the Holy Spirit, they'd be running all over the world, proclaiming the Good News of the Kingdom. And the Angels knew they would have their hands full protecting the Apostles, then us, for the next two thousand years, or more. Praise You, Jesus for those Angels.

***The Angel told Joseph to take
the Holy Family and go into Egypt***

***Statue of St. Michael the Archangel which is housed in the
silver and crystal case on the Altar in the Cave of St. Michael,
Monte S. Angelo, Italy***

St. Michael's Cave and Mountain

In our first book, *This is My Body, This Is My Blood, Miracles of the Eucharist*, we talked about **Holy Clusters.** We asked you to consider the concept of God as a Pilot flying high above the earth. From His vantage point, He can see great distances, and occurrences that are about to happen, and have already happened. Aboard *His* plane, we can see the pattern, He has created. We see clusters of holy places and events that seem to have no connection, other than that they were all instituted by Our Lord, and they are located geographically close to each other. The chronological sequence may be centuries apart. But time is a limitation put on man, not on God.

An example of clusters of holy places would be the area around Loreto, Italy, where the Holy House of Nazareth is located. Down the Adriatic coast, a short distance from Loreto, is a town called Macerata, site of a Miracle of the Eucharist, as well as a very special Shrine to Our Lady.

If we continue farther down the Adriatic coast, we come to Lanciano, site of the oldest known Miracle of the Eucharist[1] in the history of our Church. Lanciano is also the scene of a *second* Miracle of the Eucharist.

At the very heel of the boot of Italy, also on the Adriatic coast, is San Giovanni Rotondo, home of Padre Pio for over fifty years of his priesthood. Here, he received the visible Stigmata and bore the wounds of Jesus for fifty years. San Giovanni Rotondo is about twenty miles from *Monte St. Angelo*, where the Archangel Michael appeared towards the end of the Fourth Century.

---

[1]See chapter on Lanciano in book: *This is My Body, This is My Blood...Miracles of the Eucharist.*

Michael-Angel of God

St. Michael is a *powerful* Angel of God. He is our symbol of strength, power, courage and hope. Mentioned by name in three places in the Bible, Daniel 10:13-12:1, Revelation 12:7, and Jude 1:9, in each of these instances, he is doing battle with Satan. His name is actually Mica-El, which means *"Who is like God?"* That was his battle cry as he fought the battle against Lucifer and the fallen angels.

Michael is referred to in many other passages, when not by name, by rank and title. In Exodus, when Moses is leading his people out of Egypt, it is Michael, under the title of "The Angel of the Lord" who guards and protects them. It is implied that it was Michael who released Peter from his chains, and led him out of prison, as described in the Acts of the Apostles. It is also held by many that the Angel who wrestled with Jacob was Michael.

In our own Church History, Michael has always been highly visible. Prior to Vatican II, the prayer to St. Michael was recited at the end of each Mass, with the prayers at the foot of the altar. At funeral Masses, we pray that Michael will bring the soul of the deceased to the Father. *"Deliver them from the lion's mouth, that hell engulf them not, that they fall not into darkness; but let Michael, the holy standard-bearer, bring them into the Holy Light."*

From this prayer, we believe that Michael is responsible for bringing souls up from Purgatory to Heaven. There is an inspired belief that most souls are released from Purgatory on Christmas Day, that our sweet Mother Mary, Queen of the Angels, personally goes to Purgatory, to bring those who are ready to meet her dear Son Jesus to Heaven. Part of that tradition is that *Michael* accompanies our Lady to Purgatory to accomplish this joyful task.

Michael is always connected with Mary.

In all the paintings of the Holy House of Nazareth being carried to Loreto, Italy, by the Angels, St. Michael is always pictured in the lead, his red cloak flowing in the wind, guiding the house on its path[2].

In 1916, the year prior to Our Lady's extraordinary appearance to the three children at Fatima, an Angel, the Angel of Peace, came to them, and prepared them for her visit. He gave them the Eucharist[3]. One of Michael's titles is "*Angel of Peace.*" It is generally accepted that it was Michael who visited the children.

While the Angel who accompanied St. Catherine Labouré into the chapel in Paris, appeared to be a child, it is believed that he was St. Michael. It was in this chapel that Our Lady gave St. Catherine the image of the Miraculous Medal[4].

Michael is known and venerated over all the world.

Michael is Patron Saint of *Belgium*. His image can be seen on the national currency. In Brussels, Belgium, there is a huge church named after him, with a large statue of Michael on top of the steeple.

Constantine the Great had a vision of St. Michael, and had a great Shrine built in honor of the event in a town outside of Constantinople. He named the town *Michaelion*. It is located in Sosthenion, about fifty miles south of Constantinople. It has been the scene of many physical cures and conversions. Today, that whole area is part of Turkey, largely inhabited by *Muslims*. But pilgrims continue to go there to pray, and miracles are still happening.

---

[2]See chapter on *The Angels and the Holy House*
[3]See chapter on *Fatima and the Angel*
[4]See chapter on *Angels and the Miraculous Medal*

In Paris, in the midst of sinful Montmartre, the Basilica of the Sacre Coeur, (Sacred Heart) stands tall, with a huge statue of St. Michael on top, defeating Satan with his sword.

St. Joan of Arc, co-patroness of France, and a very powerful woman in our Church, testified that one of the voices she heard was St. Michael the Archangel[5]. He gave her the battle plans she carried out to save France.

In the northwestern sector of France, in the early eighth century, St. Michael appeared to the Bishop of Avranches, France, and claimed a mountain, which has become known as Mont St. Michel (the Mountain of St. Michael). In this chapter, we will be sharing the *Cave of St. Michael* in Gargano, in southern Italy, and the Mountain of St. Michael, *Mt. St. Michel*, in northwestern France.

Michael - Defender of the Church

The sound of the battle cry, "**Mica-El**" (who is like God?) can be heard echoing through the galaxies, bouncing from star to star, down through the ages, ricocheting off every corner of the earth. He is still warring, as he did when Satan and the fallen angels rebelled against God. His cry, "Who is like God? now attacks those heresies that would have us believe *we* are gods. The names are different, but the enemies are the same; as Paul said...

"Put on the armor of God, that you may be able to stand against the wiles of the devil. For our wrestling is not against flesh and blood, but against Principalities and Powers, against the world rulers of this present darkness, against the spiritual forces of wickedness on high."(Eph 6:11-12)

Michael the Archangel is Defender of the Church, Angel of God, Angel of Peace, Protector of the faithful, Archenemy of Satan and all the evil powers roaming the earth seeking the ruination of souls. Michael is famous for

---

[5]See chapter on *Saints and the Angels*

rallying the forces of the good Angels against those of the fallen angels. We see paintings of St. Michael hurling them down into the fiery pits of hell. And this great battle that took place before the earth was formed, is still going on.

Michael is someone we can call on when we feel the modern-day world of Lucifer swallowing up so many good and unsuspecting brothers and sisters. There are times when we feel as if we are walking through a holocaust; chaos and destruction all around us, threatening to envelope us, when suddenly we feel covered by a warm, protective shield. To us, that shield is our St. Michael, given to us by the Lord, to turn to, when things get rough.

We share all this with you to get you ready for the Shrine we are about to visit, one of the most famous of the Shrines to St. Michael, the Cave of St. Michael in the Gargano, at the boot of Italy. But it's also to give you a little background on this most important, most powerful Saint of our Church. As you can see, we have a great love and devotion to St. Michael, the Archangel. Our grandson Rob took the name of Michael as his confirmation name, as his grandfather, Bob, proudly stood by, as his sponsor.

There is a prayer our Ministry says before we travel, regardless of the distance. When we are on Pilgrimage, before we take off to visit the Shrines, we ask our Pilgrims on the bus to join us in this prayer. You might like to join us right now, as we pray:

Dear Lord Jesus, we ask you to send all the Guardian Angels to form a protective circle around this (car, plane, boat), with St. Michael the Archangel in charge. St. Michael in front of us, St. Michael in back of us, St. Michael to the left of us, St. Michael to the right of us, St. Michael above us, St. Michael below us. We ask for Our Lady of Guadalupe to cover us with her Mantilla, and Our Lady of Loreto (Patroness of Air Travelers) to sit on top of the (plane, car, boat) with the Holy House and the Infant

*Jesus.   We ask that anything that would harm us
physically, spiritually, emotionally or mentally be kept
away from us, and that we be brought to our final
destination to glorify Your Son's Name.*

†

The Cave of St. Michael

The Shrine of St. Michael in the Gargano was the *first*
monument of the Archangel's that we ever visited. We pray
that Michael and his Shrine touch you in the same way they
have touched us, as we have been called back, again and
again. Come with us now, and experience the Kingdom, the
Glory and the Power of God as shown to us through His
Angels, especially the Prince of the Angels, our Michael.

Around the year 490, a lord of the Gargano was
searching for one of his prize bulls. He almost gave up,
judging the bull was helplessly lost, when he spotted him in a
cave, kneeling. The cave was high above the lord, and
hopelessly inaccessible. The bull would never be able to get
out; so, as a gesture of mercy, the lord shot an arrow toward
the bull to put the animal out of its misery. The arrow
changed its course in mid-flight, like a boomerang, and
struck the lord.

The lord went to the local bishop, declaring what had
happened. The bishop immediately instituted three days of
fasting and prayer to be done *outside* of the Cave, as he was
not sure if it was a *Heavenly* inspired occurrence, or from the
other place. While the bishop, his priests, and the lord were
on the Gargano, praying at the mouth of the cave, St.
Michael appeared to the bishop, and declared:

*"I am the Archangel Michael, and am always in the
presence of the Lord. This cave is sacred to me; it is of my
choosing. There will be no more shedding of bull's blood.
Where the rocks open widely, the sins of man may be
pardoned. That which is asked here in prayer will be*

granted. Therefore, go up the mountain and dedicate the grotto to Christian worship."

The bishop apparently was not convinced that the apparition was truly the Prince of the Heavenly Hosts, or he could not have hesitated in obeying the command. The bishop hesitated *with "should I, shouldn't I,"* for two years!

The nearby town of Siponto was being invaded by pagan hordes. It was certain that the town would be defeated. Gargano was right in the path of the invaders. If Siponto fell, it was pretty definite that Gargano would go, also. The bishop asked for a three day truce for prayer.

During this time, St. Michael appeared to the bishop, *again.* He promised, if the people would attack the enemy *believing* victory would be theirs, walking in faith, he, Michael, would lead them to victory. The townspeople advanced boldly. A sand storm assailed and whipped the enemy, blinding them; huge pellets of hale joined in, pummeling them relentlessly. Terrorized, they retreated from Siponto, leaving the area forever.

The bishop climbed up the mountain to the cave. He did not come down for a long time. He seemed to be agonizing. He did not enter the cave, but instead prayed outside, at the *mouth* of the cave . When he came down, the bishop still did not have a church built there, where the faithful could worship. We don't know what caused the bishop to hesitate this second time.

There was an anguish that didn't leave him, a *gnawing* inside of him, eating at him. The cave and the Archangel's words were constantly on his mind. His spirit was being wrenched by a tug-of-war. He was being pulled in opposite directions. He knew he should be honoring the Angel's request. In his *heart*, he knew it was truly St. Michael who had appeared to him both times. But, in his head? Well, something or *someone* was holding him back.

The following year, as the anniversary of the apparition drew near, the bishop appealed to the Pope for guidance and direction. The Pope ordered the bishop to go to the cave, with other bishops and priests from the area, for three days of prayer and fasting. He was to ask the Lord for discernment, and the Angel for help. The bishop prayed *outside* the cave, at the *mouth* of the cave, again *not* inside. During this time, Michael appeared to the bishop, a *third* time. He *ordered* the bishop to enter the cave:

> *"It is not necessary that you dedicate this church that I myself have consecrated with my presence. Enter and under my assistance, raise prayer and celebrate the Sacrifice of the Mass. I will show you how I myself have consecrated that place."*

The bishop finally did as the Archangel Michael dictated. When he entered the cave, he found a splendid altar covered with a red cloth and a crystal cross upon it, as the Archangel had foretold. At the entrance was the imprint of a child's foot, confirming the presence of the Archangel[6].

A structure, which appears to be a church, was built over the cave. From the street level, one can see towers, and arches, and bells. Actually, it's only a facade. Pilgrims have to walk down 86 steps to the cave, which *is* the church. It was set up as a church, with an altar rail, pews, and side chapels. Over the years, an *Episcopal* (bishop's) chair was carved out of a huge block of stone and placed at the side of the altar. Chapels were hewn lovingly out of local stone and placed in the cave. It was even raised to the level of a *Basilica!* It is known as the *"Celestial Basilica"*; maybe because the church has never been consecrated by a bishop

---

[6]In the chapter on *The Angels and the Miraculous Medal*, we speak about Our Lady's apparition to St. Catherine Labouré in the chapel of the Miraculous Medal in Paris. The Angel who brought Catherine into the chapel took the form of a child, and it is said that it was St. Michael, the Archangel.

(nor have any relics been placed in the altar stone). It has been consecrated by the presence of Michael, himself.

The Cave of St. Michael *immediately* became a famous Shrine for pilgrimages. At one point in the Middle Ages, there were four major Catholic Shrines in the world. They were called: **Deus** (or God) for the Church of the Holy Sepulchre in Jerusalem; **Apostoli**, for the tombs of the Apostles in Rome; **Sanctus**, for the Shrine to St. James, called Santiago de Compostela, in Spain, and **Angelus**, *for the Cave of St. Michael*, in the Gargano in Italy.

The history of the Shrine is not only most unusual, but also a great tribute to, and affirmation of, the power our Lord Jesus has given to His Angels, especially His Prince of the Heavenly Hosts. Michael has protected the Shrine from the earliest days. It really gets interesting, as we go down through the ages. The whole world was constantly either attacking or under attack, being conquered by this one and that one. Italy was occupied by many foreign invaders. The Shrine of St. Michael being where it was geographically, the Greeks were in control of the area for quite some time, as were the Longobards[7]. At one point, the Saracens conquered the little area. But then the Carolingians[8] felt it their duty to free the little town from the infidels.

Here's the exciting thing. All these rulers who came in and conquered this part of Europe had a great devotion to St. Michael the Archangel. They considered him almost like their own patron saint. He was definitely the Patron Saint of their armies. They believed it was a great honor to be able to protect this special Shrine. *Some regarded it as a mandate from God!* In addition, they spent time and money, building the Shrine. But, as each new conqueror came in, he built over what had been done by his predecessor. At any given

---

[7]or Lombards, from Lombardy - Germanic tribe from the Po Valley
[8]Family of kings, descendants of Charlemagne the Great, or his grandfather, Charles Martel.

time, the Greeks, Saracens, Longobards, Carolingians, Swedes, French (Charles of Anjou) and the Spanish (Aragonese) were in control of the mountain, and were paying their respects to the mighty Angel, and his Shrine.

The way this all came about was that the Shrine became so popular so quickly, its prominence spread immediately to every part of the known world of that time. Michael has always been a favorite of royalty; as the story of the Shrine spread, it was embraced by kings and heads of armies. We pray that the reasons for the many conquests of the area had no connection with the victor's desire to possess the Shrine to the Archangel, for their own glory. Whatever the reason, at a point in history, it was given the title of Principality, and was dubbed "*Onore di Monte St. Angelo*", or the Honor of the Mountain of St. Michael.

St. Michael has always honored this holy place, which he claimed for himself and the Angels. Proof of his ongoing protection of the mountain occurred when the entire area was besieged by a plague in 1656. The townspeople were falling victims to the plague when the Bishop of the time, prayed to the Archangel for his help. He enjoined all the people of the area to join him in prayer and fasting. On September 25, 1656, the Archangel appeared to the bishop.

"*I am the Archangel Michael*" he said. "*Anyone who uses the stones of this grotto will be liberated from the plague. Bless the stones, sculpturing upon them the Sign of the Cross and my name.*"

The bishop did as the Angel ordered, and the plague left the area. The bishop praised the Lord, proclaiming to all, the miracle was through the intercession of His powerful Angel, Michael. This gave rise to a tradition which exists to this day. Pilgrims still come to the cave of St. Michael, wanting to take little stones with them. Nowadays, it's actually forbidden to take them without permission.

It's really good that not too many people know about the tradition. The cave could have been stripped completely of its stones, if the many overzealous pilgrims knew about it. To give you an idea of how misguided we, the faithful, can be: the tree where Padre Pio fought off demons as a young man, in Pietrelcina, has been completely stripped; the holmoak tree where Our Lady stood when she appeared to the children of Fatima, was completely destroyed by overzealous pilgrims. Perhaps here, they're afraid the mountain will collapse, or worse, the Angels will get them.

That may sound funny, but the local people take the Shrine and the presence of the Angels very seriously. Penny and I have been visiting the Shrine since 1976, when we went on our first pilgrimage. With the exception of 1978 and 1987, we have been to this Shrine at least once every year.

We have knelt at the altar rail for hours, just to take in the majesty of St. Michael. There is a beautiful statue of the Archangel[9] above the main altar, perched on top of the spot where his footprint was seen by the Bishop in the 5th century. The statue is lighted, enclosed in a silver and heavy crystal case. St. Michael is resplendent, lovingly represented by the magnificent statue of him, carved of the finest carrera marble. He wears a gold crown, wields a gold sword, high above his head, ready to strike at Satan. On the tip of his pinky, he has a gold chain which wraps around the serpent's neck. Michael is holding Satan at bay, with disdain, and ease. Is Michael telling us that we are to remember, *he* thrust Satan out of Heaven? When we feel under unbearable attack, whether of mind, body or heart, we must remember we always have the great Defender of God, Michael the Archangel.

---

[9]The statue of St. Michael was carved out of carrera marble by a well-known sculptor, Andrea Contucci, better known as Sansovino

St. Francis and the Cave

The Cave of St. Michael was not only an important Shrine for the royalty; it was a Shrine for the *saints*, as well. They felt impelled to visit. It was a great honor to spend time at the cave of St. Michael. Some saints who came to venerate St. Michael in his cave were: Sts. Anselmo, Bernard of Clairvaux, William of Vercelli, Bridget of Sweden, Gerard Maiella, and our very special Poverello, St. Francis of Assisi.

The story of St. Francis brings distinctive respect to the Angel and his cave. St. Francis had a particular devotion to the Angels, and especially St. Michael. Each year, he would celebrate what he called "*St. Michael's Lent*". It ran from the Feast of the Assumption of Our Lady, August 15, to the Feast of St. Michael and the Archangels, September 29th. He prayed and fasted the entire time, almost 45 days. During one of these Lents, Francis received the Stigmata.

But that is in another chapter of this book[10]. Here we want to talk about a pilgrimage Francis made to the Cave of St. Michael during St. Michael's Lent one year. He came and prayed outside the cave for thirty days and nights. At the end of that time, he did not feel worthy to enter the cave, so he carved the Franciscan **T** (tau)[11] on a stone, and left it outside the cave. He departed, and never did enter the cave.

A chapel was built in honor of the visit made by the Poor One of Jesus, because of his great respect for the Angels of God, and his unbelievable humility. A fresco was painted above the altar, which is showing signs of age. It shows St. Francis, and in back of him is an image of Saint Lucy.[12] This is in honor of the blind man who was given sight by the intercession of St. Francis.

---

[10]See chapter on *The Saints and the Angels*
[11]Cross in the shape of a Greek T - symbol of Franciscans
[12]on the right, as you face the altar

Above: ***Pope John Paul II praying before the statue of St. Michael in the Cave***

Below: ***Cave of St. Michael on Monte S. Angelo, Italy***

The Angel's Pardon

When you have descended all 86 steps, and have arrived at the entrance to the cave, you see a doorway with huge carved bronze doors. The two doors are divided into twenty four panels. On the left are episodes where the Angels were involved in the Old Testament; and on the right are representations of the apparitions of the Angels in the New Testament (6 panels): the Angel's appearance to St. Lorenzo Maiorano (three panels), to St. Martin of Tours (two) and the sixth panel has an inscription in which the donor entrusts himself to the protection of the Archangel and to the prayers of the faithful. Carved on the arch which surrounds the massive doors is written the *Angel's Pardon*, given to the bishop on the occasion of the third apparition:

"Where the rock opens widely, there the sins of man are forgiven. This is a special place where any fault is washed away."

As we enter the mouth of the cave, we feel a profound humility. The Lord has allowed us to return. Here, we can once again ask the Archangel to petition the Lord for His Pardon. We often take with us, *spiritually*, those who cannot come on Pilgrimage, begging the Archangel to intercede for them, asking the Lord to grant them the same forgiveness of sins, so they may have peace, the peace that only reconciliation with the Lord can bring about.

The Angel's Pardon is not meant to bypass or supersede confession, the Sacrament of Reconciliation. Indeed, one of the most active ministries of the Benedictine priests at this Shrine is the Sacrament of Reconciliation. Padre Pio used to send penitents to this Shrine to pray to the Archangel that their hearts might be opened, so that when they returned to San Giovanni, they might make a good and full confession.

A tradition of our pilgrimages is to hold a Penance Service, the night before we go to the Cave of St. Michael. Very often, it's in conjunction with a Holy Hour we have at the original church of Padre Pio, in San Giovanni Rotondo. We believe that the thrust of the Angel here is to focus us on the sins we have committed, to repent our sins, and to experience the grace of Our Lord Jesus through the cleansing Sacrament He has given us. We believe the Angels and Saints work very closely for our well-being and salvation. Padre Pio was a strong proponent of Reconciliation. The Archangel Michael in this cave brings to the forefront of our consciousness, the need and value of *Reconciliation* with God. We believe the Angels and Saints don't really care which of them we give credit to, as long as we are in communion with God, so that He can heal us. As you recall, before healing people, Jesus first said "*Your sins are forgiven you.*" The Lord was saying without that unity, in love and trust in God, there can be no healing.

Why have Our Lord Jesus and His beautiful Mother Mary given us these Holy Clusters, places not connected chronologically, but by the powerful presence of the Divine Family? Why did Padre Pio come here in 1917, fourteen hundred years after St. Michael had claimed the entire region? Was it to bring people's attention back to this powerful Shrine? Is it a coincidence that the most powerful force of both Shrines is Reconciliation? Was Jesus trying to tell us something through these two related incidents, fourteen hundred years and twenty miles apart? We know the Lord doesn't work with coincidence, unless it's *Holy Coincidence*. Don't we?

†

The Mountain of St. Michael

Again, we speak of Holy Clusters. Mont St. Michel (Mountain of St. Michael) is located on the far end of *Normandy*. Nearby is Pontmain where our Lady of Hope[13] appeared in the year 1871, bringing with her appearance the

---

[13]written about in "*The Many Faces of Mary*"

miraculous retreat of the German Army and the end of the Franco-Prussian war.   Her message of *hope*: *"But pray, children. God will soon answer your prayers. My Son allows Himself to be touched."* is as relevant and important today as it was then. We need hope! We need to know that our Lord is listening and that through prayers, and His Mother's intercession, He will give us another chance.

On the same coast is Dunkirk where hundreds of thousands of American, British and German lives were lost. When Bob, Rob and I went there, on the fortieth anniversary of the D-Day Landing, in 1984, I couldn't remain in the museum they have of artifacts from that battle. The most horrible part of the experience for me was the screams and crying out of the men. As we looked down the cliff, at the sheer drop to the beach below, we realized the only way the Allied forces landed was by the sacrifice of many lives, those who were the first off the landing crafts.   Again, sacrifice! *When are we going to accept our Lord's ultimate Sacrifice and stop killing one another?*   Maybe, when the whole world knows our Savior, and when we, who do know Him, begin to live more purely the Gospel He left us.

Less than one hundred miles, on the other side of Normandy, is Lisieux, home and Shrine of Saint Therese, the Little Flower.   Something interesting, and we would say miraculous, is that when Lisieux was badly bombed, during the Normandy invasion, neither the house where Saint Therese and her family lived, the Convent where she wrote her *"Autobiography of a Soul,"* and as a Carmelite Nun spent nine of her twenty-four years, nor the Basilica built in her honor, were touched. We know that, as a cloistered Nun, Saint Therese never left the *Carmel* (the convent). But we also know she earned the title of co-patron Saint of the Missions and Missionaries. How was she able to reach Missions thousands of miles away? We definitely believe, her intercessory prayers to our Lord were responsible; but could it be that the Angels, in addition, transported to those in need, the *confidant assurance* required to live each day?

The History of Mont St. Michel - 708 A.D.

When the miracle occurred, in 708, the whole area, which is now a bay, was a forest. Two rocky peaks broke the massive forest. One was and is still called Tombelaine and the other was known as Mont Tombe. Mont Tombe, or as it is now called Mont St. Michel, was once a Shrine to Belen, the *Celtic god of Light*. It later became a Shrine to the Roman *Mercury*. It did not become a Christian place of worship until the 5th century, when it was occupied by hermits from the other side of the channel (somewhere in the British Isles, as it is now known, probably from Ireland). They set up two oratories under the protection of Saints Stephen and Symphorien.

In 708 A.D. the Archangel appeared to St. Aubert who was then Bishop of Avranches. Michael commanded that a Sanctuary be built on Mont Tombe, in his honor. And so, the Sanctuary was built on the very mount where the pagans worshiped. This is not unusual in the history of our Church. In Assisi, for example, there is a church called *Santa Maria Sopra Minerva* (Saint Mary over the temple of Minerva). It is fitting for the Church to do this. Did not Saint Paul go to the pagan Gentiles and bring the Good News of Jesus to them, very often using their pagan beliefs to help them understand that the god, they believed in, was no match for the One and Only God.

When you visit the Shrine, you have to stop and wonder *how* they were able to do it, first to fight the strong pagan influence that still prevailed and then the physical difficulty? But when God is in charge "cannot a child, with the Angel's aid, cause the monuments of a pagan cult to tremble?"

Saint Aubert sent representatives to Monte Sant Angelo (Cave of Saint Michael) in the Gargano, Italy, to retrieve a relic from the mountain. When the emissaries returned with the precious stones from the Holy Cave, what did they find, where there formerly had been a forest, but, waves smacking upon the shores of a sea-swept bay. *The forest had become an island!* Do you find that hard to believe? Well, how do you explain this? This is not only the tradition of the Shrine, but *geologists* have confirmed that in the eighth century, a sudden encroachment of the sea did take place around the new Christian Sanctuary that was there. Phenomenon, or as we would rather believe, *miracle?* We, for our part, believe in miracles. But for those who do not, no explanation is possible.

The miracle of changing the forest into an island created its own set of problems, when it came to constructing the buildings on the island. Many workers died, bringing materials over to the island. They had to carry huge, heavy block across the sea to the mountain. Often, the material was so heavy, the carts and animals sunk in the marsh. But the Lord would have His way. With Michael and the Angels in charge, the monument was completed.

The new college of twelve canons, founded by Saint Aubert, were custodians of the Shrine for two hundred and fifty years. In 966 A.D. it was taken over by the Benedictines whom Duke Richard I, Duke of Normandy, judged more worthy of the task. New buildings were added and old ones repaired, but the real reconstruction period began in 1017, under the new Duke Richard II. He ordered it begun after his marriage was celebrated on Mont St. Michel.

The laying of the foundations for the crypts, which would eventually support the mass of church buildings on the island, was in itself a miracle. Remember, in those days, they could not blast into the mountain. They did not have derricks to lift the heavy stones used to build the many churches and buildings. But build they did.

In 1154, the mount became known for more than buildings made of stones and mortar. With the new Abbot of Mont St. Michel, the building became *spiritual*, with the introduction of an impressive collection of manuscripts which the new Abbot composed and transcribed, himself. The Mount became known as *"The City of Books."*

But often, good works, even sometimes *holy works*, suffer the ruthless attacks of the fallen angels. This great period of prosperity and enlightenment, during which the Benedictine Abbey's fame spread widely over the continent, was soon to be ended with a series of disasters. In 1203, Bretons joined forces with others to attack the Mount. Though the occupants of the Abbey resisted the invasion, many buildings were damaged in the onslaught. The Abbot, after the battle, ensued the aid of one of the former invaders who had since become Duke of Normandy, and not only were the buildings restored, but others added. In the 13th century, fortifications were put up to insure against invasion.

In 1423, these precautions were to prove they were not made in vain. Another attack! Abbot Robert Jolivet, one of those associated with Joan of Arc's trial, having been won over by the English, sought to capture the Abbey. It was heroically defended and once again, remained in the hands of the custodians. One of its loyal defenders sent this message back to the English, *"Tell your master that we are resolved to hold this place for our legitimate sovereign or to be buried in its ruins."* According to the accounts of that time, the Archangel Michael raised a miraculous storm whose fury wrecked the majority of the English ships, dashing them against the rocks at the foot of the Mount.

Although the enemy had a blockade formed around the Mount, the custodians did not capitulate and held on to the Mount, resisting bravely for the next ten years.

In 1469, the Order of St. Michael was established by Louis XI and the Abbey became the headquarters of the Order, gaining new renown.

The Mount was again to know strife, its peace attacked by the *Wars of Religion*. This time, the attackers were frenchmen, Hugenots. The monks defended the Abbey against the unrelenting bombardment, refusing to surrender, until 1595 when Henry IV converted to Catholicism.

Pilgrims of the Middle Ages were replaced by sightseers. If that was not enough of an affront to the Archangel Michael, monarchs began to use Mont St. Michel as a *"Bastille of the Seas"* where political prisoners were *detained* for the amusement of the royalty's pleasure.

The French Revolution did not ignore the Mount. The bells stopped tolling, as the mad mobs rushed through the Abbey and churches, destroying everything in their wake. For the first time, the Mount was unable to resist, and they were forced to capitulate. The Abbey buildings were turned into prisons, the first inmates, *three hundred priests* who had too freely opposed the *new order*.

Napoleon III, by Imperial decree, did away with the penitentiary of Mont St. Michel, protesting vigorously against the manner in which the famous Abbeys in France were being treated and for what purpose they were being used, condemning those who *"had changed into shameful prisons and haunts of crime and the most monstrous vices, what had once been the havens of mercy and of learning."* A new respect for the Mount came about.

Today, when we visit Mont St. Michel, we go as pilgrims; but sadly, most come as tourists interested in the Mount as an *eighth wonder of the world*. One reason they come might be because they have read about unexplainable occurrences such as, twice a month the tide comes in, making of the Mount, an island. (Author's note: If you've parked in the parking area at that time, you may find your car under water the next morning.) And then, with no rhyme or reason, the tide goes out the way it came in. Geologists have not been able to explain how or why this occurs. They often are so in awe of the phenomena, they miss the miracle. And in missing that miracle, they miss the great miracle, the Archangel's message that he is present, fighting the enemies of God and His children. Like Jesus, he echoes across the bay, "Be not afraid!" Michael is always with us. Praise Jesus.

Mont St. Michel

The Annunciation of Gabriel to Mary
"Let it be done unto me according to your word."

Mary and the Angel Gabriel

God created the world and He was pleased with what He created. He was delighted with the sky, the seas, the mountains, the fish, the animals, and most of all, His latest creation - man. How well they got along with one another. Then God, in his Infinite Love, believed man should not be alone; he needed a partner, and so He took a rib from the side of Adam and created Eve. God thoroughly enjoyed watching them. He had created them to be happy, and they were until......

The serpent saw Eve in the garden and he tempted her. Our Lord had created Adam and Eve with a free will. That was not free to sin, but to love! The enemy tells us just the opposite. And he told Eve the same lie he is telling so many today, the lie that is as old as Satan himself: *"You don't need anyone. You are god, the master of your own fate. You only go around once. Take care of yourself. Let the rest of the world take care of themselves."* And oh, how we buy into that lie; so, do not judge our first parents Adam and Eve.

He told Eve, "You can be like God. You can possess all the knowledge of God." *Pride*! "Don't listen to God. He doesn't want you to be as smart as He is." *Disobedience!* "Go ahead, you deserve it!" *Selfishness*! Satan called God a liar! How did Eve not know what he was trying to do? The all-loving God Who had created them, Who asked nothing in return, how could she have believed this lie about God? Like the Angels before them, they had an opportunity to believe and obey God and have everlasting life, or believe and obey the liar, the serpent. At that moment when Eve said yes to the devil, the world as God had planned it, changed. All the lunacy, the waste of God's Creation, the inhumanity of man to his fellow man would never have happened. God planned for us, as after Christ's second coming, that the lamb lie down next to the lion, without worry that the lion will betray him and eat him!

When did Eve sin? When did it all begin? Was it when she gave the apple to Adam to eat? Or was it when she continued to listen to Satan, knowing she was betraying the trust the Lord had placed in her and her spouse Adam? Did she not know that a *yes* to the one (Satan), would negate the *yes* she had made to the Only One, Her Lord and God?

When the Angels were created, the Lord gave them an opportunity to choose Him once and for all, or to choose against Him. Satan chose to go against God, and with his lies and false promises led other angels to follow him. They say that, if given a choice, no one would leave Hell. Satan chose the life he leads and has never been sorry. He made an irreversible decision and there is no turning back for him. He is so angry with God, he will do anything to cause Him pain. And how can he cause God pain, by leading us away from Him.

The new Eve

As one woman Eve was sinning against God, losing eternal life with the Father, He already had in His Mind another, *Mary*, who, with her obedience, would bring to the world, a Savior. God said the Woman would crush the head of the serpent. Satan, the serpent heard this, and so he waited! But whom God chooses, he protects with His Army of Angels.

In the New Testament, we hear first of the Angel coming to Zechariah.

"Do not be frightened, Zechariah; your prayer has been heard. Your wife Elizabeth shall bear a son whom you shall call John. Joy and gladness will be yours, and many will rejoice at his birth; for he will be great in the Eyes of the Lord...He will be filled with the Holy Spirit from his mother's womb...I am the Angel Gabriel who stands in

attendance before God. I was sent...to bring you this good news."

Gabriel comes to Mary

There was a buzz of excitement in the air. For the Jewish people, the promise of a Messiah, given to them from before the time Moses had led them out of the desert, was imminent.

There was a great need for the Messiah. God's people had been in bondage before, but now, the Romans had completely suppressed them. The pagan influence of the captors was creeping into the beliefs and lifestyles of the sons of David. There was no pride left in the Jewish people, only the memories of King David and King Solomon. They needed another David, another Solomon, someone who would deliver them from their enemies, and give them back their dignity.

It was into this setting that the young girl, Mary, had grown up. She grieved for her people, not so much because of their physical suffering, but because they were losing their faith in Yahweh, Abba, their Father, to take care of them. They were looking to *man* for answers, and Mary knew there would be no help coming from man. She prayed her people would look to their God for deliverance, trusting that He would hear and answer them.

Hers was a life of prayer. She had been consecrated to the temple as a child. Her ongoing prayer was that the Messiah would come in her lifetime, and free the people she loved so much. Although she spent much of her time in the temple, since her father's death, she watched over her aging mother. While she was at her home in Nazareth, she prayed constantly, even while doing her chores.

It was late afternoon on a March day. She had just returned from the well, after having drawn water for her house. As the sun went down, a chill crept into the air. She knelt in her room, praying. She fantasized on how it would be like when the Messiah arrived. Was it fantasy, or prophecy?

On a parallel course, in another dimension, God's dimension, the golden gates of Heaven opened, and one solitary figure emerged. It was an Angel; it was Gabriel, God's special messenger. The time had come for Gabriel to announce the Lord's merciful decision to send to earth His Son, the Messiah, to change the course of salvation history. Gabriel began his descent to the earth.

While Mary prayed, the wind stirred throughout the room. She thought it was just the winds blowing off the sea, cooling the house. But then she could feel an electricity in the air. She looked around. There was nothing. Suddenly a great calm came over her. The wind stopped. The figure of a beautiful young man manifested himself before her eyes. There was a brightness about him, as if he were translucent. He looked at her. His eyes were brilliant. At first, she was frightened; then a rush of warmth came over her whole body. She couldn't take her eyes from him.

"Hail, most favored one. The Lord is with you." the young man proclaimed. She was startled by his words.

"Don't be afraid, Mary; you have found favor with the Lord. You will conceive in your womb, and bear a Child, and you will call Him Jesus. He will be great, and will be called the Son of the Most High, and the Lord God will give to Him the throne of His father David, and He will reign over the House of Jacob forever, and His Kingdom will have no end."

Mary's mind was reeling. Who was this man? What was he talking about? How could she conceive and bear a child? She was a virgin. She wasn't married! She was engaged to Joseph the carpenter, but they had vowed to live a celibate life as husband and wife. None of this made any sense. Yet while she wondered, she never doubted. She asked him with excitement and wonderment, as a child would ask her daddy how an impossible task would be accomplished.

"How can this be, since I am a virgin?"

He answered,

"The Holy Spirit will come upon you and the power of the Most High will overshadow you and for that reason the Holy Child to be born will be called the Son of God."

She gasped. She didn't understand at that moment what the messenger meant by the Holy Spirit coming upon her. The key word in her mind, in her entire being, was *"The Son of God."* Is this man speaking of the Messiah? Is he telling me I am to be the mother of the Messiah, the Son of God? Am I the one I've been praying for, the one to be the vessel to bring Salvation into the world? Is that what he's saying?

The Angel further affirmed the power of God. He added,

"And behold, your cousin Elizabeth in her old age has also conceived a son; she is in her sixth month, and everyone thought she was barren. You see, with God, nothing is impossible."

Mary prayed for a long time. Oh, my Lord, it *is* You. Is this really possible? Would you give this honor to me? I'm not worthy. But the words of the Angel pierced her consciousness, *"You see, with God, nothing is impossible."* I trust you, my Lord and my God. I know you would never hurt me. And I would give up my life for you.

She looked up at the Angel before her? He was waiting for something, what? Was this messenger of God waiting for an answer from her? She looked at him again. He *was* waiting for her yes! Tears streamed down her face. He looked at her with so much love. She could feel the warmth of his gaze.

For a moment, time stood still. Heaven and earth waited with baited breath for the answer to come from Mary.

The Angels halted any movement, and concentrated on their prayer. They prayed with all their might for the virgin to give the correct answer to God.

"*I am the handmaiden of the Lord. Let it be done unto me according to your word.*" And as the tears cascaded down her cheeks, she cried out in her heart, "*Yes! I say Yes!*"

In her mind, she could hear choirs of *Angels* singing praises to the Lord. The *Angel* before her, whom we know to be Gabriel, looked at her with such joy in his eyes. A brilliant light shone in the room, and surrounded her. She felt a surge of energy go through her body. She looked up at the Angel. He looked at her. He smiled. It was done.

The *Angel* slowly disappeared, and the room became dark. The little girl, now woman, sat in the darkness, her heart beating, her mind racing. She repeated silently, the words of the Angel. She was to be the Mother of God. She could feel *His* presence inside her. It was true. Now she understood all.

What went through Mary's mind, when the reality of what had happened came crashing down on her? She had said yes; she was now pregnant. She had a heavy burden to carry; but we believe the Lord gave her the strength and courage to handle it. God doesn't make mistakes. He knew before the beginning of time that this child would be the pivotal point, bringing mankind from the condemnation of Adam to the Salvation of Jesus. And she was to be the instrument. She was the happiest woman in the world. She was highly favored of the Lord. Her Magnificat, chanted some few weeks later, in the presence of her cousin Elizabeth, confirms the abounding love she had for her God, Who had blessed her so.

But it wasn't going to be all roses. There was that problem of how to tell everyone, especially her mother, Anne, and her betrothed, Joseph, what had happened. We have to believe that Anne knew her child had been born for specialness. The circumstances around her birth were proof of that. Anne most likely believed Mary's account of what had happened to her, immediately.

But then there was Joseph. Mary loved him dearly. Although he was much older than she, there was a bond between them that was so strong. He had always trusted her completely. She looked at his eyes as she explained the events of the Annunciation. He was sad; he was hurt; he didn't believe her. What bothered Mary most, having hurt Joseph, or the fact that he didn't believe her? How do you feel when someone you love very much, your very best friend, doesn't believe you? It's devastating. It must have been that way for Mary.

But she persevered. She trusted in her God. She knew He would not abandon her. There was a physical as well as spiritual link between her and the Almighty. As much as she grieved, seeing Joseph as he suffered pain and sorrow, she couldn't help but be so happy when she felt the warm glow of the God Who was growing inside her. She knew that God had given her a most powerful Angel to protect and guide her through this journey of faith. He would make all things right, which he did.

Gabriel came to Joseph in a dream, and confirmed Mary's story to him. He told Joseph it was all right to take Mary as his wife. We know that Joseph was relieved. He loved Mary. How could he help but love her. With the exception of her Son, she was as perfect a human being as the world would ever know. In another chapter in this book[1], we go into detail, the relationship between Joseph and the Angel Gabriel, which carried him through his life.

The overpowering message for us in the Annunciation is Mary's *"Yes!"* She recognized the Angel; she knew he came as God's messenger, as Scripture had taught her. The

---

[1]See chapter on *Jesus and the Angels*

Lord through His Angel gave her an impossible proposition, and she said "Yes." She had faith in God, that no matter what happened, He would make it right. She could stand on that faith. She staked her life on it. Do we trust God in proportions anywhere near those of Mary? Do we listen to His *messenger*, even when we *know* he is from God? Do we give over control to God, and then take it back at the first sign of adversity? Or do we cling to control over our lives until we get into a problem situation we just can't handle, and then turn to God for help?

Mary didn't say very much in Scripture; but every word out of her mouth was a gem. If we were to sum up the teaching of the Annunciation, words to live by, it would be Mary's word to the Angel Gabriel. She knew he represented God and so, without reservation, she abandoned herself completely to the Lord with:

"Let it be done unto me according to Your Word."

Our Lady of Pilar[1] and the Angels

There is no doubt in any of our minds that if the Lord chose, He could do anything and everything He wishes without the help of His Mother Mary, the Saints or the Angels. When Jesus walked the earth and died for the sins of man, He showed the powerful *humility* of God. He came to us, born of *human* estate, a helpless, vulnerable, totally dependent *Baby*. He made Himself dependent on the love and the care of two humans, His Mother Mary and His adopted father Saint Joseph.

As we walk through the history of Salvation, the *Angels* play a key role, often bringing to the prophets of old, God's message of love and hope. The Lord uses Holy Scripture to send His consoling Word: "*Fear not...Be not afraid, I go before you always...I will be with you until the ends of the world,*" 365 times, once for every day of each year of our lives. Why not use the Angels to bring the Good News that there is nothing and no *one* to fear! I am sure it did not appear *so* to many of those to whom they came.

After our Lord died on the Cross, we know, it seemed to be all over. The Apostles and disciples ran and hid. They were without hope. All their dreams of a Messiah were gone; they had died on the Cross with Jesus. Alone and discouraged, without a Leader, they were lost. They stood huddled in a room. And all the while, an *Angel* was there at the tomb of Jesus, giving Mary Magdalene the Good News: Jesus had Resurrected and with Him, they too.

We know that after the Holy Spirit descended upon them, the Apostles set out to live and *yes*, to die for the Lord. James left for Spain soon after the Ascension of our Lord, to bring the Good News of Jesus to the Gentiles of Spain, fulfilling the Words of Jesus, "*The last shall be first.*"

---

[1]Pilar is Spanish for Pillar - our Lady's title is Our Lady of Pilar

Jesus appears to His Mother-He tells Her: Go to St. James

Mother Mary left, we are told, to go and live with St. John the Evangelist, to whom Jesus had entrusted His Holy Mother (*She is your mother*). According to Sr. Mary Agreda, in "*The City of God*," our Lady was in Ephesus when our Lord Jesus appeared to His Beloved Mother and asked her to go to Spain, to console and encourage Saint James in the path the Lord would *now* be asking him to follow.

According to an ancient and venerable tradition, our Lord sent His *Angels* to accompany and transport His Mother and their Queen to visit Saint James in Zaragoza, Spain where he was staying at the time. Her mission was to tell Saint James that the Lord was pleased with the work he had been doing, evangelizing the people of Spain, but that *now* his Lord's desire was that he return to Jerusalem to be martyred[2].

The tradition of the Shrine, for almost 2000 years, has been that our Lady was carried on a cloud by *Angels* to Zaragoza. The following events are chronicled to have taken place on the night of January the 2nd, 40 A.D. While they were traveling, carrying their precious Passenger, the Angels were industriously carrying a pilar of marble and carving a miniature image of our Lady.[3]

We can only wonder and dream what our Lady was thinking, as she floated over this land, her Lord and God had created. Did she smile as she looked down upon the towering mountains of Italy housed in an unlikely looking boot. Did she see beyond the colorful, peaceful-looking, patch work farms of France to the struggles this eldest daughter of the Church would suffer? Did she catch her breath as she looked upon the plains of Spain so handsomely framed by mountains on one side and the sea on the other?

---

[2]According to Sr. Mary Agreda, given to her by our Lady in an apparition, as written in "*The City of God.*"
[3] same as footnote 2

Was she dreaming, musing a little? Would her Son be soon calling her Home to Heaven to be with Him? According to the tradition of Sr. Mary Agreda's *"The City of God,"* our Lady was 54 years old, at this time. It was approximately 13 years before she would be Assumed by her Son into Heaven. Her mission was to bring Jesus' command to Saint James to return to Jerusalem to be martyred. What had been her martyrdom? Was *Hers* the dry martyrdom Archbishop Fulton Sheen spoke of? He said, *"Wet Martyrs"* shed their blood for the Faith. *"Dry martyrs suffered over a period of years pain that far exceeded that of the brief interval of the Wet Martyrs.*[4]*"* He cited that each day, hour, and minute of their lives was a Profession of Faith.

We know Mary loved the Apostles, especially St. John to whom she had been entrusted. She had been given Saint John as a son, but he could not take the place of her most perfect Son Jesus. Ask any mother who has lost a child; oh, she loves all whom the Lord sends her, but no one can fill the emptiness, no one can replace the piece of her heart that was ripped away when her child died.

Her merciful God had kept Mary quite busy since her Son died, affirming, encouraging, bringing new hope and instilling more courage when the Apostles wanted to run at times. Had her Son left her behind, to keep the family of Christ together? When we read the Acts of the Apostles, we get a small glimpse of the dissension and the division often brought about by the misunderstanding Lucifer and his fallen angels tried to cause, to try to split up this holy and chosen family, our first Bishops and Priests. Was she thinking that this journey might be her last mission on earth?

Was our Lady smiling as she arrived in Zaragoza? What did she see as she glided gracefully toward the little

---

[4]from chapter on Archbishop Fulton J. Sheen in *Saints and other Powerful Men in the Church*

Left:
While they were traveling, carrying their precious Passenger, the Angels were industriously carrying a Pilar of marble and carving a miniature image of Our Lady

Bottom:
Altar and original Church built by St. James and the Angels

Right:

Our Lord sent His Angels to accompany and transport His Mother and their Queen to visit Saint James in Zaragoza, Spain.

Left:

Saint James and his disciples were deep in prayer. Their hearts almost burst at the sight of their Mother Mary and her Heavenly Escorts!

village of Zaragoza? Saint James and his disciples were deep in *prayer*. What got their attention first? Was it the bright light of the *Royal Entourage* whose rays cut through the dark of night? Was it the heavenly voices of the Angels, chanting hymns in honor of our Lord Jesus and his Mother Mary? Had St. James and his disciples shot up from their knees? Or did they awaken as if from a dream? Or did they judge they were still dreaming?

For *what* had they been praying? I am sure, it was pre-empted always by the Will of the Lord; but did they feel the Wind of the Holy Spirit at their backs, knowing He wanted more of them? But *what*? How their hearts must have almost burst at the sight of their Mother Mary and her Heavenly Escorts! Did tears rise up in their throats as they saw before them the evidence of how very much their Lord loved them? He had sent His Mother to them!

Did they sit at her feet? Was she mounted on a throne of heavenly clouds, the Angels' wings fluttering happily around Her? As she spoke, were the sounds of the Angels singing the Gloria to God, softly accompanying her, in the background? Did it seem like an eternity until she spoke? Did her eyes fill with tears of joy as she looked at *this* son of hers who would be soon going Home to be with his Lord, her Son Jesus?

"James, the Lord, My Son has brought you a message through Me. You are to return to Jerusalem to be martyred." *To be martyred?* Did Saint James wonder of what use it could be, his being martyred? Had he been praying for his next mission? *And this was it?* But, we know he said *yes!* Did our Lady have to hold out one of her delicate hands to keep Saint James from rushing out to do her Son's Will before he knew the Lord's full and complete plan for him?

Build a church in honor of Our Lady and her Pilar

Our Lady went on. Before leaving for Jerusalem, our Lord wanted Saint James to build a church on this very site where she was now appearing to him. Her image, so carefully molded by the Angels on their Heavenly pilgrimage, was to be mounted on top of the pillar, the Angels had transported. It was to be part of the main Altar. This done, our Lord would bestow special graces and protection upon the people of Zaragoza, in exchange for their pure devotion to our Lord and to our Lady.

Our Mother Mary remained with them until the church was completed. Although it is not written, you can be sure the Angels did not stand idly by and watch human hands *alone* do the work of bringing honor to the Lord and His Mother. After the last rock was laid and the roof of the new church completed, our Lady left with her Angels.

Saint James leaves for Jerusalem

Saint James followed soon after, taking his last journey, only now into Jerusalem to be martyred, in the name of Jesus. We write in this book a little about Guardian Angels. As Saint James journeyed in faith toward his beloved homeland, Jerusalem, to be martyred, was he not sustained by his Guardian Angel?

Words like martyr and *martyrdom* sound so romantic and they do make inspiring reading. But if we are not careful, as we read about the *many* who shed martyr's blood for this beloved Church of ours, we can lose sight of the cost, the courage, the faith and the total abandonment to our Lord's Will it took for them to say yes to this extraordinary act. We can begin to take *them* and their *gift* to us, the Body of Christ, for granted. *And* if we are not alert, we can be deaf to perhaps what the Lord is asking of us *today*.

If we are not aware of that Angel who is always with us, to guide, to light and to protect us on our way, we might try to do it all by ourselves. Oh, we might do good things, but the minute *we* do it, not the Lord through His Angels and the intercession of his Saints and His Mother, then we get into trouble and begin to be fooled by the thought *we* are the masters of our own fate and destiny. Like with our first parents, Adam and Eve, we might buy into Satan's lie. Our spiritual director once said that when *Pride* comes in the door, it is wide open for the other vices to easily enter.

We have heard it said that when a prophet, or a priest, or a founder leaves a place, if the work started by him does not live on, it was *his* work and not the Lord's. In the case of the people of Zaragoza, they began *immediately* to celebrate Mass at the little church built by Saint James, his disciples and the *Angels*. In addition, they began to treasure and venerate the holy image left by Mary and her Angels at the same time. And they continue to do so, *right up to this day*.

Pope John Paul II and Our Lady of the Pilar

The pilar that had been fashioned by the Angels is still there and has been venerated and kissed by the faithful for almost *2000 years*. When you visit the Chapel of our Lady of Pilar, you will see the tiny image resting on the Pilar brought over by Mother Mary and the Angels. And if you go to the back of the Chapel as our Pope John Paul II did, you too can kiss the Pilar.

On November 6th in the year 1982, when our beloved Pope John Paul II pilgrimaged to this holy Shrine, he knelt, like the millions before him and kissed the holy Pilar. He celebrated Mass at the Chapel of our Lady of Pilar, built by Saint James and the Angels 2000 years before. He prayed to his Lady, to the one to whom he has pledged his all (Totus Tuus), only now before her image and title of Our Lady of *Pilar*. On that day, Pope John Paul II, very moved, and with great emotion, removed his zucchetto from his head and left it and a beautiful rosary, as a remembrance of his visit. The following are some excerpts from the Pope's address to the Faithful in Rome:

"In my spiritual Pilgrimage of today, I wish to direct my thoughts to the Virgin of the Pilar in Zaragoza, Spain, whose basilica I had the pleasure of visiting, fulfilling my wish of kneeling as a devout son of Mary before her sacred Column. This venerable Shrine, built on the banks of the Ebro River, is a great symbol of the presence of Mary since the beginning of the preaching of the Good News in the Iberian Peninsula.

According to an ancient local tradition, the Virgin appeared to James the Apostle in Zaragoza to console him, and she promised him her help and maternal assistance in his works of Apostolic preaching. Even more, as a signal of protection she left him a marble Column that, through the centuries has given the Shrine its name. Since then, the Pilar of Zaragoza, as it is commonly called in Spain, is considered as the symbol of the firmness, the constancy of the faith of the Spanish people and moreover, it is also an indication of the road that leads to the knowledge of Christ through the Apostolic teaching.

The Spanish Christians have seen in the Pilar a clear analogy with the column that guided the people of Israel in their pilgrimage to the Promised Land. Therefore, through the centuries, they have been able to sing "Columnam disciples habemus," we have as a guide a Column that accompanies us to the new Israel."

Before Pope John Paul II, the Popes, right from the beginning, issued Papal Bulls attesting to the authenticity of the Shrine and Mother Mary's appearance there, accompanied by the Angels.

In the fifteenth century the newly elected Dutch **Pope Adrian VI** who happened to be in Spain, at the time, made a visit to the Shrine of our Lady of the Pilar.

Pope Pius XII elevated the church of Our Lady of Pilar to the honorable title of *Minor Basilica*.

Cardinal Roncalli who would later become the unforgettable **John XXIII** also visited and venerated the Pilar and the image of our Lady of Pilar.

But it has been said that no Pope has gone as deeply into the true significance and *importance* of the Pilar in the local as well as in the Universal Church. The people of Zaragoza have proclaimed, that, more than any other Pope, John Paul II can be called truly *Pope of the Pilar*. He has made four visits to the Shrine, two of which were *personal*.

Veneration to Our lady of the Pilar began 12 years before she was Assumed into Heaven.

Think about it! The people of Spain were venerating the Mother of God under the title of *Our Lady of the Pilar* for at least 12 years before she was Assumed into Heaven. As we said, according to Sr. Mary Agreda[5], our Lady was 54 years old when this miracle occurred. We are also told in *The City of God* that our Lady was assumed into Heaven when she was 67 years old. Her apparition in Zaragoza, 12 or 13 years before our Lady's Assumption, was the only one we know of that took place during her lifetime.

The little church, built 2000 years ago is still the same. Only they soon began building a larger church over it to accommodate the thousands that grew into millions of pilgrims that journey there each year. It is an awesome sight to behold, and it does take your breath away, when you enter this towering church dedicated to our Lord through His Mother Mary. But when you kneel in the Chapel, before the holy image of Mother Mary, receive her Son our Lord in the Holy Eucharist, and go to the back of the Chapel and kiss the pilar transported by the Angels, that's when, as with

---

[5] same as footnote 2

Bob and me, you fall apart, as do the thousands of pilgrims who have gone with us.

Did our Lord need His Mother to go to Saint James to bring him His message to return to Jerusalem to be martyred? We believe not, because we know He is all powerful and can make His Will known in any way He chooses. But the truth is, He has been using His Mother since before this time to now, to do just that.

Did our Lady need the Angels to transport her to Saint James? Why could she not have bi-located[6] as many of the Saints who have followed Her? We believe she traveled like the Queen she is, with her *Royal Escorts*, as befits the greatest Queen who ever lived. And also, to teach her children that we can go through life alone, falling and rising and falling again, or journey as she did, as sons and daughters of the King of all, as princes and princesses on the way to our heavenly kingdom, with *our* Heavenly Escorts.

The Spanish people, every day at every hour, sing to their Patroness the traditional invocation:

"Blessed and praised be the hour in which Blessed Mary and the Angels came in mortal flesh to Zaragoza."

---

[6]Bilocation is the actual presence of one finite person in two places at the same time.(The Catholic Encyclopedia)

***Angels Transporting the Holy House of Nazareth across the
Adriatic Sea to Loreto, Italy***

The Angels and the Holy House

We believe the Lord uses His Angels to do the *extraordinary*. He has great power, and He has given the Angels *some* of His power that they might glorify His name, and help us in our walk toward Him. While we agree that God formed nature, and adheres to the rules He has set up for nature, we also believe God can do *anything* He wants, *whenever* He wants. We contend it's wrong for humans to put God into a box, making the decisions as to what He can and cannot do. If God, in His majesty, wants to set aside the laws of Nature, and give Angels bodies with wings, and superhuman strength to pick up large objects, like houses, and transport them at the speed of light anywhere He chooses, we say Yes, Lord, praise You Lord, thank You Lord. Jesus said, "*I assure you, if you had faith the size of a mustard seed, you would be able to say to this mountain, 'Move from here to there,' and it would move. Nothing would be impossible for you.*" (Matt:17:20)

Do I believe God can move mountains, and with faith I can? Yes, because He told me so. Do I believe God, through His Angels, moved the Holy House from Nazareth to Italy? Yes, because I have seen it. Do I believe God can move men's hearts? Now, I shout *yes* from the mountain tops because through prayer, I have experienced it.

Our Lord Jesus loves His Mother Mary. He watches out for her, and protects everything on earth that had anything to do with her time here. And so it was, in the year 1291, when the Saracens (Moslems) decided to vent their venom and hate against Christ, and all things Christian. The Crusades were over. The Christians had been defeated and run out of the Holy Land. By destroying every holy place in Palestine, the Moslems thought they could eliminate every sign or vestige of Jesus' existence in history.

St. Helena, Emperor Constantine's mother, had made churches of all the holy places in Jesus' life. It was as if the

Saracens believed, if they took away these outward signs of Jesus, they could wipe away that Love that beats in each and every person's heart, that longing to *be* more, to love and be *loved* more. We wonder, were the Saracens the ones who really wanted to destroy man's hope, or could it be it was the fallen angels who know all too well the needs and desires of the human heart?

The Saracens went on a rampage. There would not be a stone left upon a stone on any of the holy places. If there were no longer any shrines where Jesus was born, where He grew up, where He taught, where He healed and called man to new life in His Father, where He died for us, where He rose giving us eternal hope that we, too, would rise, then man would forget he has a Savior, and have no reason to live. Satan was having a field day. He could see the last remnants of Christianity *destroyed* in this Holy Land.

The Saracens descended on Bethlehem. They went to the church built over the spot where Christ was born. They would level it! But when they approached the building, there was a mosaic outside, depicting the three wise men. This could not be the place of Jesus' birth, they thought. *This is a mosque, dedicated to Arab kings of the past.* So they left this place, and continued looking for the birthplace of Jesus. Our Lord had used the Angels to form a shield around the church, which blocked the minds and senses of the Arabs. He would not allow this place, where His Mother had given birth to Him, to be desecrated.

At about the same time, hordes of Arabs rode, for all they were worth, their horses covered with foam of white lather as they strained to go beyond their limit, towards *Nazareth*. They would destroy the house of Mary. Never again would Christians celebrate the Annunciation, there. Never again would they be reminded of the Jewish Virgin's *yes* that helped to redeem the world. It was well known that Jesus' Apostles and disciples began celebrating Mass in the

Holy House of Nazareth soon after Jesus' death. It was a shrine from the earliest days of the Christian movement. This was an important place for the Saracens to destroy. *This is where it had all begun.*

We believe there has always been a legion of Angels protecting the house of the Annunciation. Here, Gabriel appeared to Mary, and the Holy Family lived until Jesus began His public ministry. We believe Gabriel never left this place. But now, when danger seemed so imminent, we can visualize an *army* of Angels racing down from Heaven, their wings glistening in the sun, Michael joining Gabriel, his red cape whirling around him. The sky was filled with Angels, from one end of the horizon to the other. The earth shook with the vibrations of their wings. They swooped down and formed a barricade around the house. The Angels were here, and they meant business!

Our Lord had good reason to call forth His Angels. The Basilica, built over the Holy House, had been destroyed *twice* before by the Arabs, once as long ago as 1090 A.D. For some *unknown* reason, they had never disturbed the crypt (lower church), where the Holy House and the grotto were located. The Crusaders rebuilt the Basilica shortly after they arrived in Nazareth. Acts of sacrilege by the Moslems, were a major reason the Crusades began in the first place; for it was right after the atrocity to the Basilica of the Annunciation that the Holy War began.

The *second* time, the Basilica was destroyed, was in 1263. Again, the crypt was not disturbed, praise God. But then, the Crusaders were not able to rebuild the Basilica, and the Holy House was left unprotected. When it was evident the Crusaders had lost the Holy Land in 1291, our Lord Jesus decided that since He could not depend on *man* to protect this holy place, He would send the Angels. *They* would surely defend this shrine to His Blessed Mother and their Queen. The Lord gave the Angels a mandate!

"Move the Holy House; take it to a safer place, far from the hatred of My enemies in this land of My birth. Lift it; lift it high into the air, where they can't get at it. Don't let them see it."

We can be sure Michael and Gabriel were in charge, supervising the movement of this most holy place, where the Holy Spirit had formed the Savior of the world in the womb of Mary. In unison, the Angels raised the house from its foundation, and carried it high into the sky, resting it upon clouds which hid it from the earth. When the Arabs arrived, with hatred in their hearts, craving to pillage and burn, they were astonished. There was nothing there! Only the grotto remained. They left it alone; it had no meaning to them.

The Angels transport our Lady and the Holy House

The Angels carried the Holy House, high above the mountains and deserts of the Holy Land, across the expansive Mediterranean and Adriatic Seas to *Yugoslavia*. On May 10, 1291, it landed in the quiet little hamlet of Tersatto, in Croatia, Yugoslavia, far from the battle cries of Palestine.

It was early in the morning, when the local people discovered, to their great surprise, a house resting on the ground. *There was no foundation under it*! Curious to see what it was, they ventured inside. They found a stone altar. On the Altar was a cedar statue of Mother Mary standing with Her Divine Son in her arms. The Infant Jesus had the two first fingers of His Right Hand extended in a blessing, and with His Left Hand, He held a golden sphere representing the world. Both Mary and Jesus were dressed in robes. Golden crowns were poised on both their heads.

The villagers were awestruck, but *confused*, until a short time later, our Lady appeared to the local priest and said,

"Know that the house which has been brought up of late to your land, is the same in which I was born and

The Altar inside the Holy House of Loreto with the statue of Our Lady

brought up. Here, at the Annunciation of the Archangel Gabriel, I conceived the Creator of all things. Here the Word of the Eternal Father became Man. The Altar which was brought with this house was consecrated by Peter, Prince of the Apostles.

"This house has come from Nazareth to your shores by the power of God, of Whom nothing is impossible. And now, in order that you may bear testimony of all these things, be healed. Your unexpected and sudden recovery shall confirm the truth of what I have declared to you."

The priest, who had suffered for years from an illness, was immediately cured. He promptly told all the people, and word of this Gift from God, spread throughout the countryside. Pilgrimages began coming *immediately* to the Holy House of Nazareth, in Yugoslavia. God had chosen to bring it to this little village, and the villagers lovingly responded by erecting a modest, quite primitive building over the house, to protect it from the elements.

However, the joy, the Croatians had experienced at having this most precious gift in their midst, was short-lived. Three years and five months later, on December 10, 1294, the Holy House disappeared overnight from Croatia, never to return. Saddened by the loss, Nicholas Fangipani, a devout man from Tersatto, built a small church, a replica of the Holy House, on a hill where the original had stood. He placed an inscription:

"The Holy House of the Blessed Virgin came from Nazareth on the 10th of May, in the year 1291, and left on the 10th of December, 1294."

The people from Croatia continued venerating our Lady in their replica church. So great was their devotion that Pope Urban V sent the people of Tersatto an image of our Lady in 1367, which was said to have been carved by St. Luke, the Evangelist.

The Angels move the Holy House to Italy

December 10th, 1294, in the area of Loreto, *Italy* (across the Adriatic Sea and southwest of Tersatto,) shepherds reported seeing a house in the sky, flying across the sea, supported by Angels. They reported, one of the Angels (Michael) wore a red cape, and seemed to be leading the others. They saw our Lady and the Baby Jesus seated on top of the house. The Angels continued inland, about four miles, and landed with their precious house and its Royal Passengers into a wooded area called Banderuola.

The news spread, quickly drawing many people to pilgrimage to the House in Banderuola. But they were not all working on the same agenda. Robbers came to waylay, rob, and beat the pilgrims. The faithful stopped coming, and the house quickly fell into neglect.

The Angels, who had been put in charge of protecting the House, lifted it *again* and set it down on a small *hill* in the middle of a farm. The only problem was, this land was owned by two brothers, named Antici, who began fighting immediately over ownership of the house.

So the Angels moved the house, a *third time*, to another hill. They placed it in the middle of a road, the site it occupies now, and has for the last 700 years. Tradition tells us that as soon as the house moved off the brothers' property, they became the best of friends. The Angels had moved the Holy House *three* times in one year.

The people of Recanati and Loreto didn't know exactly what they had there. They knew it was a church, and it had appeared miraculously. They knew about its movement, from place to place, the first year it was there. They'd heard reports of the multitudes of miracles taking place as a result of praying at the church. *That* was about as much as they knew. But in 1296, that was all to change. Two years after it had landed in Loreto, our Lady appeared to a very holy man,

Paul of the woods, a hermit. She explained the origin of the house, and concluded with these words,

"It remained in the city of Nazareth, to the great consolation of Christians until, by the permission of God, those who reverenced this Holy House were expelled from the city by the arms of the infidels. And since no honor was any longer paid to it, and it was in evident danger of being profaned by the infidels in contempt of the Christian name, it seemed good to my beloved Son to translate it from Nazareth to Illiria (Yugoslavia) by the hands of Angels, and afterwards, to remove it to your land."

Paul of the Woods took the story to the people of Recanati, who, being aware of the miracles that had taken place at the House, sent a group of sixteen men, first to *Tersatto*, and then to *Nazareth*, to check out the authenticity of the House. The team of experts took with them, all the measurements and full details, of the House in Loreto.

Experts set out to verify the authenticity of the Holy House

The team's first stop: *Tersatto*. The villagers verified, indeed, that the House had been there and (as with the House in Loreto) it had had walls of a reddish colored stone and were about sixteen inches in thickness. When they measured the facsimile that had been built in Tersatto, in remembrance of the Holy House, they discovered that *it measured the same as the Holy House in Loreto* - thirty-one and a quarter feet long by thirteen feet four inches wide by twenty-eight feet high. They spoke of it having one door which, again as in the House in Loreto. was seven feet high with a four and a half foot wide *opening*. It too, had had *one* window. They described the earthenware vessels that the Italians, too, had found in the House. Their depiction of the statue of the Holy Mother and the Infant Jesus could not have been more perfect.

The investigators went on to *Nazareth*. There they would discover whether the House was really that of the *Annunciation*. The measurements of the *foundation*, in Nazareth, were *exactly* the dimensions of the *House* in Loreto and the *facsimile* that had been built in Tersatto. After a period of about six months, the investigators returned to Loreto, and affirmed the *authenticity* of the House.

In the years that followed, more inquiries were made. They found coins beneath the House, not only from the area of Nazareth but also from the period it resided in the Holy Land. Stones and soil, used for the grouting of the house, were found to be identical with those found in Nazareth, from that level of civilization.

When you journey to the Holy Land, you can still visit homes very similar to this house of the Holy Family. In Nazareth, people still live, like the holy carpenter and his Family, in modest one room homes where they eat as well as sleep. They have only one cupboard, just as Mary had, to keep cups and plates. As you look at her cupboard which is still in the Holy House in Italy, to the left of the altar, it is difficult to come to terms with the truth that in this humble, unpretentious house, the *True* Royal Family, our *Holy Family* ate and slept, prayed and shared, were Family!

As we brush against the ancient stone walls of the House, we can almost touch Mother Mary as she goes about her duties as *a Wife*, a faithful one. As our eyes travel to the window (the Angel's window), across from the altar, we can hear Mary, the *Daughter*, obeying the Will of Her Father. We can cry and laugh, hope and pray with *our Mother*, a loving, caring and protective Mother. Sometimes a Sister, sometimes a Mother, always a Friend, Mary is so *touchable*, so *one* of us, so *like* us in all things except in sin. We could spend days at this shrine, just meditating on the importance of this house in our lives, as we dare dream and walk through the thirty years Jesus spent here.

As the Holy House became a popular place for pilgrims, a traffic problem developed. Typical of houses of that period, and often even now, there was just one opening, at the side of the house. When the pilgrims tried to exit, they would have to fight to get out, because of the crowds pushing and shoving to get in. Many were nearly crushed. Pope Clement VII decided to close the original door and have *three* doors built. He commissioned a famous architect to do the job. There may have been a problem, however, in that no one asked *our Lady* for permission. When the architect took his hammer to make the first break in the stone, his hand withered, and he began trembling, helplessly. Regaining his strength, he *fled* from Loreto, never to return. After this, *no one* would go near the job.

When the situation looked the dimmest, a cleric named Ventura Barino volunteered to do the job. He and his workmen *fasted and prayed* for three days, before beginning the work. On the third day, Barino went up to the wall, fell to his knees and prayed to our Lady. His prayer went something like this,

"Dear Lady, I'm innocent. It's not really me striking this wall, but the Pope. He's doing this so that your Holy House will be more accessible to those people who would venerate you here. So, if you are not happy with this task we are about to undertake, I would really appreciate it if you would take it up with the Pope, and not me."

With that, the men began the remodeling, which exists till today. You can still see the wooden beam that had been over the Holy Family's door. The original opening was filled with stones removed from areas of the house where the three new openings were made.

Because of the enormous number of Pilgrims coming to the shrine, the people of Loreto believed certain precautionary measures needed to be taken. They would have to brace the structure; they judged the house would not be able to support the *weight* of the pilgrims. In addition, they would have to preserve the Holy Building from the weather. *So*, they covered it with a brick wall! But after the work was completed, the wall *separated* from the Holy House. In the excavations, beneath the House, there is enough room, for a boy to walk between the House and the wall they had built. You can also see that the house does not, till today, rest on a foundation.

If you are having a problem believing a house can fly, can be transported by Angels; if, like a woman who overheard us telling about the Holy House in the Super Market, you believe God can move mountains but not houses, then how would you explain a house without a foundation, if it wasn't *miraculously* set down by Angels? One thing, we *know*, and I am sure you agree, you cannot build a house without a foundation. If the Angels did not transport the Holy House, how do you explain it *being here* without a foundation? The only way you could have a building, without a foundation, is if someone set it down.

Restore to the Virgin what has been taken away.

A bishop from Portugal visited the Shrine of our Lady of Loreto. He thought it would be a *terrific* idea to take a stone from the wall of the Holy House, bring it back to Portugal, and build a church over the relic, in honor of our Lady of Loreto. The priests at the shrine refused. However, the Pope gave his permission. The Bishop left his secretary in Loreto, to remove the stone, while *he* went to Trent.

Mission accomplished, stone in hand, the secretary began his trip, to rejoin the Bishop in Trent. The Bishop suddenly became ill. As the secretary advanced closer to

Trent, the Bishop's health worsened. By the time the secretary arrived, the Bishop was near death. The Bishop sent word to the local Nuns to pray for his recovery. Two days later, he received word.

"Our Lady says, if the Bishop wishes to recover, let him restore to the Virgin what he has taken away."

The bishop and the secretary were stunned. There was no way the Nuns could have known, except through Mary.

The secretary left immediately for Loreto with the stone. As he got closer to Loreto, the bishop's health became better. By the time the stone was returned to its rightful place, in the Holy House, the bishop was completely healed. As a result, the bishop sent a letter to Loreto prescribing severe penalties on anyone who would attempt to remove any of the stones from the Holy House. His letter is still in the archives at Loreto. Over the centuries the Popes have prohibited, under threat of *excommunication*, the removal of any part of the Holy House, for any purpose.

The holiest place on earth

The Holy House is considered, *"The holiest place on earth."* Blessed by the Holy Family Who lived there, and the Angel Gabriel who appeared there to Mary, it was chosen, not only to provide shelter and bring Good News then, but, for all time.

Before the Holy house left Nazareth and was transported to Loreto, St. Francis of Assisi told the brothers, they were to open a house in Loreto. When they questioned him, arguing the town was too small and remote, he prophesied,

"Someday, it will be known as the holiest place on earth."

When Francis went to evangelize the Holy Land, he visited the Holy House, there. Had Mother Mary told him of the move that would take place after he was with her and her Son in Paradise? For centuries, the custodians of the

Holy House have been obeying their Seraphic Father, faithfully, lovingly caring for the Shrine and spreading devotion to our Lady of Loreto and Her Holy House.

For centuries, the Holy House of Nazareth, in Loreto, has been a favorite shrine for Saints, those Beatified and Popes. Hundreds of Saints have visited the Holy House, including St. Thérèse of Lisieux, St. Maxmilian Kolbe, St. John Bosco, St. Francis de Sales, St. Teresa of Avila, St. Dominic Savio, St. Frances Cabrini, St. John Neumann, St. Alphonse Liguori, to mention a few. Over 200 who have been canonized, beatified or declared venerable by the Church have come and prayed at the Holy house.

Saint Maxmilian Kolbe stopped there on his way back to his City of the Immaculata, in Poland. Did our Lady give him the strength, there, that he would need as he faced the cruel and inhuman treatment of the Nazi soldiers in the infamous concentration camp, Auschwitz?

Saint Therese had gone to Rome to appeal to the Pope for permission to enter the Carmel at age fifteen. She visited the Holy of House of Loreto on that pilgrimage. Did our Lady, as she did in Cana, ask her Son to change the bishop of Lisieux's mind as He had changed the water into wine?

St. Francis de Sales took his vows of celibacy in the Holy House.

Throngs of Popes have come to Loreto. They supported the Holy House, issued Papal Bulls affirming it, and granted special indulgences to the faithful who venerate the Blessed Mother in this Holy Shrine. Sometimes they even aided, financially, the construction work of the Basilica.

Pope John XXIII came to Loreto, the day before he convened the Second Vatican Council, and asked our Lady of Loreto to protect and guide the Council. It was the Feast of St. Francis, October the 4th, 1962. Little did the smiling, jubilant people who cheered their beloved Pope know that within one short year they would no longer have him with them, on earth.

A photographer snapped a picture of our Pope with the statue of our Lady of Loreto in back of him, and she was smiling! Never before, or since, has anyone taken a picture of the cedar statue of our Lady *smiling*. Was she smiling, knowing she would have Mother Church victorious, no matter what attacks and pains she would suffer because of misunderstandings and division over Vatican Council II? Was she smiling because she knew, with Vatican Council II, there would be an explosion of the Holy Spirit, and the laity would take their rightful place beside the priesthood and the religious, and the Church would *bloom*?

The late Pope *John Paul I* came as a cardinal, as did *Pope Paul VI*. And now, our Pilgrim Pope, *John Paul II* has come as Pope *twice* to the Holy House, spending much time praying and I am sure listening to his Lady, pledging, as always, "*Totus Tuus*," all yours, Mary.

For the local Catholics, the Holy House of Loreto is a place where the most important events in a person's life can be gauged. It's like a *parish* church for Catholics in a hundred mile radius. They come to be baptized in the Holy House, to receive First Holy Communion, be Confirmed, to be married; and then, when the Lord has called them Home, to be buried from there. It is definitely a shrine of social status. Everybody wants to be able to say they did something important in their life at the Holy House.

It has always drawn *us* back. We began visiting that shrine in 1977, and have continued to go back at least once a year, but most often twice or three times with pilgrims. For us, the Holy House of Loreto is the scene of the Annunciation. As we look up to the Angel's window in the Holy House, we are reminded it was from this window, the Angel Gabriel appeared to Mary and proclaimed: she was chosen to bring the Son of God into the world. It was in this room, she would give that big yes that would change the course of history. As we lean against these walls, she brushed against, as she tended Jesus and His adopted father St. Joseph, we dare to ponder what *yes* the Lord might be asking of us!

Loreto is a very small village, of no importance other than the *greatest*; the *Holy House of Nazareth* blesses its ground and its people by being there. It overlooks the breathtakingly beautiful Adriatic Sea. And off in the distance, you can almost see the land from where it came, seven hundred years ago, Yugoslavia. We could stay there for days and days, drinking in the love of our Lord Jesus, Mary and the Angels, that comes not only from the Holy House, but spills out into the *piazza* with its push cart vendors and friendly local citizens who line the picturesque streets. Going back there, is like going back to your old home town, where you were born and grew up. After you're there a few minutes, it's as if you had never left. Maybe, it's because *Mama Mary*, who always makes and brings family together, is there, *waiting*. We have never had a pilgrim tell us, this was not one of the *highest* points of their pilgrimage, if not *the* high point.

Pilgrims, for *centuries*, have prayed the Rosary, circling the House, on their knees. There has never been a time, we have been to the Holy House, that we have not encountered the *Faithful* passionately reaching out to the Mother of God, believing she will answer them. And they come. And they pray. And Jesus answers them: "*Be not afraid; My Mother has pleaded for you.*" The ruts, their shoes have made in the marble platform around the house, are evidence of the devotion and *testimony* of the response to that devotion, by our Lady. The rosaries said, as they painfully process on the marble ledge on their knees, echo throughout the church blessing other pilgrims as they too, pray.

Loreto is called the *poor man's* **Lourdes.**

During the summertime, the *White Train* arrives twice a week, bringing sick and infirmed pilgrims to the Holy House. Every evening, after Mass, the sick process out of the Basilica, their litters forming a circle around the *piazza*. They patiently, hopefully await the entrance of the Blessed Sacrament. They have come to our Lady of Loreto, to the Holy House of Nazareth, to ask for her intercession with her Son. They know, in this Holy Place, where our Lady cared for her Son, she will now ask Him to care for them, her other children.

Although they have spent much time in the little house of Nazareth, and have prayed the Rosary to our Blessed Mother, they know, because she has told them, her Son *Jesus* is the only Healer. And so their hearts swell with hope and expectation as their Lord and Savior processes in front of them. Tears of joy run down their faces as the Lord blesses them, through His priest as he raises the Monstrance containing the Living Lord, the Blessed Sacrament. As in Lourdes, no one leaves Loreto the same. Healings always take place, of the body, the mind, the heart and the soul.

On nights, when we have been too tired to go to the procession, the voices of pilgrims, mingled with those (we are sure), of Angels call out to us and we are on our way to the procession and the Lord's blessing.

If people *only* come to the Holy House because the Angels brought it from Nazareth, rather than for the *real* meaning of the House, that it is where the Holy Family lived, where Mary trusted and said yes to the Angel Gabriel, they will truly be missing out on the great gift the Lord and His Family have in store for them. For here, where they touched and loved, where they laughed and cried, the Holy Family still waits, to love and to touch...*us*.

When pilgrims come and enter the Holy House, whatever agenda they were on, they are no longer on. They find, instead of asking for this and that, they are overcome by the overflowing love of the Holy Family and their Heavenly hosts, the Angels, and they can do nothing but *praise* our Lord Jesus, and His Mother Mary. They are so happy for the gift, and the Giver, they can't possibly conceive that His powers would be limited. And so, they come! And so, they pray! And so, the Angels bring their love and petitions to our Lord. And so, miracles come about.

†

The movement of the Holy House, that is, it's being brought to Yugoslavia first, and then to Italy, has been documented, from the earliest days of its arrival. One thing that has always bothered us is, *why did the House move from Croatia?* We have come to know how *religious* the people of Croatia have always been, even in the face of Communist domination. We scrutinized all the reports about the movement from Yugoslavia to Italy, even Mary's statement to Paul of the Woods. All she said was *"it seemed good to my beloved Son to translate it from Nazareth to Illiria (Yugoslavia) by the hands of Angels, and afterwards, to remove it to your land."* But there's no clue *why* it was moved.

Then, we began looking through the Almanacs and history books, to see if anything could shed light on what was going on in the world, that would cause our Lord Jesus and His Mother Mary to move the House of the Annunciation across the Adriatic to Italy, at that time. We discovered that the dreaded Turks, the same Moslems who were trying to destroy the Holy House in Palestine, had *conquered Croatia*. But that was in 1526, some 229 years *later*. Then we found an old map which tracked the *Ottoman Empire*, the Turks who took over Croatia. Their great push began in *1299*, into Greece, and onward north and west, until at one point in history, they ruled much of southwest Asia, southeast Europe, and northeast Africa. Their empire covered a huge area of the world, and it wasn't until the First World War that they were finally pushed back to the confines of Turkey. There was over 600 years of Moslem domination in that part of the world, which included Yugoslavia.

We don't know for sure what the reasoning of our Lord Jesus, and His beautiful Mother Mary was, but it's very possible that this onward and upward move of Christianity's greatest enemy, the Moslems, had something to do with it. The persecution of Christians was *inhuman*. We would have to envision the black angels of hell, screeching with delight, as they led the Turks against the followers of Christ, and took over Christian Europe. The Holy House would have been a prime target for destruction. But the Angels of God swooped the Holiest Place on earth from the hands of God's enemies, in *advance*, and brought it over to Loreto, where it rests to this day.

There has never been a question that the house was transported from Nazareth by the Angels to its present location. As early as fifty years after the House arrived, there have been paintings showing the Angels flying with the House[1]. Also, pilgrims' medals were struck in the 1300's and 1400's, showing the Holy House, with the Angels supporting it, and our Lady and the Baby Jesus sitting on top. When you visit the Vatican Museum, as you walk through the galleries, if you look up, you will see on one of the ceilings, a painting, not unlike the one on our cover, of the Angels transporting the Holy House with Mother Mary and the Baby Jesus atop the House.

For us, as authors, Loreto and the Holy House is a place of *inspiration*. We could probably set up shop, and

---

[1] There are three paintings, which date back to the early 1300's, which show the Holy House being transported by Angels. One, the earliest known, is in the Metropolitan Museum of Art in New York. It is in a book called, *"The Book of Hours of Joan d'Evreux"*. The second is in the Church of San Marco, in Jesi, Italy. The third is in a Franciscan chapel in a church in Gubbio, Italy.

write our books inside the Holy House, if the custodians wouldn't throw us out. We have felt such a strong presence of Mary there. Bob felt the closest to Mary he has ever felt in his life, in the little Holy House. We were given the name of our second book, **The Many Faces of Mary**, in Loreto. We believe the Angels speak to us, at this shrine. We have received *insights* there. Many of the themes of our books come from time spent in the Holy House. We believe we are put into an atmosphere, a vacuum, where Mary and the Angels speak to us, *and we can actually hear them with our hearts*.

You don't have to go to the Holy House of Loreto to hear Jesus, Mary and the Angels speak to you. It can happen anywhere. But give yourself a treat. If the Lord wills it, go to this holy place, where the *Annunciation* took place, where the *Holy Family* lived and loved for close to thirty years, and join the Angels who have protected it for centuries, as they chime in, adoring the Lord during the Holy Mass. Open your mind and your heart to what your Heavenly Family is saying to you. Oh, by the way, if you've ever had a problem believing in Angels, and their power, it will all become very academic when you come to this place. They will capture your heart.

Above: *Apparition of Our Lady, St. John, St. Joseph and the Angels*
Below: *Pope John Paul II celebrating Mass at the Shrine*

Mary and the Angels at Knock

Mary has been given the title and office of Queen of Heaven and Earth, of all the Angels and the Saints. Therefore, it makes a lot of sense to say that Angels play a major part in anything Mary does. Wherever you find Mary, you will find Angels. The miraculous events of August 21, 1879, in the little village of Knock, in the county of Mayo, would tend to affirm this fact. And the message is really so explosive that we need Angels to be there at her side.

Angels have had a great deal to do with the history of Ireland. We believe this Holy Rock has been specially blessed by the Lord, and the Angels have been on constant duty there to protect the people and their faith. It may well have begun with St. Patrick, who is credited with having converted Ireland, back in the Fifth Century. Patrick's life is full of visions and encounters with Angels, from the beginning of his ministry, all throughout it, even to the extent of deciding where Patrick would die.[1] Is it possible that the Lord kept the Angels on duty in Ireland after the days of St. Patrick, because important things would happen in this land?

Of all the countries in the world, Ireland would have to be considered the most faithful to the Catholic Church, from the day St. Patrick converted it, to this day. Theirs is the only Christian country we're aware of, where divorce is illegal, and abortion is still not permitted. Granted, they're fighting a hard battle, with evil forces attacking them from all sides. Possibly the most devastating assault against these dear faith-filled people is coming very subtly through the Satan of television. They're weakening, but they're still hanging in there.

The people of Ireland have paid a severe price for their loyalty to Our Lord Jesus, His Mother Mary, and all the Angels and Saints. They have experienced a cruel and

---

[1] See chapter on *Saints and Angels*

inhuman persecution from their nearest neighbor, who would be considered by many as kin to the Irish. Of course, don't ever say this in an Irish pub. It's taken it's toll on the population of the country. (There are fewer Irishmen in Ireland than in Boston, Mass. There are as many sheep in Ireland as people.) The economy of the country has suffered severely because of the drain of centuries of bondage. But they are a strong people, good reason for our Lady to choose to smile on them.

On August 21, 1879, a rainy day to be sure, our Lady came to Knock, Ireland, with St. Joseph, St. John the Evangelist, a Paschal Lamb, and a *Heavenly Army of Angels*. She appeared at the back of the Knock church, and stayed there, with fourteen visionaries, for a period of about three hours, in the pouring rain. But in all that time, she never said a word to anyone, nor did she even acknowledge their being there, except when one of them got too close, fourteen year old Patrick Hill, at which point our Lady moved back away from the child. During the investigations which followed the apparition of Mary, a great obstacle was the fact that she said nothing. Till today, Knock has never been officially approved by the Church, even though two Popes have visited the Shrine, the most recent being the occasion of the 100th anniversary of the Apparition, August 21, 1979, when Pope John Paul II came as a pilgrim to Knock Shrine.

When we first wrote of Knock and our Lady's Apparition, in our book, *The Many Faces of Mary, a love story*, we thought she said nothing because she was pleased with her Irish children and their faithfulness under the worst conditions. We still believe that is true, but only part of the truth. Curiously enough, it was the Angels that made us realize what Mary was actually doing in Knock, Ireland.

One night, in New Orleans, while preparing our slides for a lecture tour of that holy state, we saw something in the Apparition at Knock that just snapped us to attention. *It was the Angels!* On the right side of the Apparition, there was an Altar with a Lamb and a Cross, surrounded by Angels. The Angels' wings were fluttering in the Apparition. We had been taught, maybe a month before this time, about St. John Chrysostom, a Doctor of the Church, one of the Early Fathers. St. John said that when the priest extends his hands over the bread and wine at the beginning of the Eucharistic Prayer, *he summons down the Holy Spirit!* You listen the next time you're at Mass. The Angels don't have the power to summon down the Holy Spirit, but our priests, by their ordination and consecrated hands, have been given that power. St. John taught that when the Holy Spirit descends upon the altar, *He is accompanied by tens of thousands of Angels, present on the Altar to protect and adore the Eucharist.*

That was it! That's what Mary was trying to tell us at Knock, Ireland in 1879. It was the Mass, the Eucharist. She was telling us to *defend the Eucharist!* Our belief in, and the importance of, the Real Presence of Jesus in the Eucharist, is under such attack today.

Then our eyes traveled to the center of the apparition, to St. John, dressed as a Bishop, holding open the Book of the Gospel. The Word; Mary was telling us to *defend the Word.* The Gospel is so fragile. It's like a crocheted sweater. If you pull one thread, the whole sweater unravels into a heap. Cast doubt on one part of the Word, and the rest will topple with it. Some people tell us Jesus did not physically resurrect from the dead. It was a spiritual Resurrection. Well, if He didn't resurrect, as it says in Scripture, was He really crucified? And if He wasn't crucified, was He really born? And if He was not really born, is there a God? So, you can see how we must defend and protect the Word with our lives.

And then, we looked to the left, at Mary and St. Joseph. In the slide we show, a lady was kneeling at the side altar, and had left her infant at the feet of St. Joseph. The Family;

we could see the Family. Mary was telling us to *defend the Family.*

Mary was speaking to us loud and clear at Knock. *Save the Eucharist,* because if you destroy the Eucharist, you destroy the Church! *Save the Word,* because if you destroy the Word, you destroy the Church! *Save the Family,* because if you destroy the Family, you destroy the Church, and you destroy the World!

Prophecy? Was Mary warning us of things to come? Was the message of Knock for the people of Ireland of 1879, or the people of the world of 1991? This past year, when we were interviewing Fr. Joseph Pio at San Giovanni Rotondo, getting background for our documentary on Padre Pio, he called our Lady of Knock - *Our Lady of the Apocalypse!*

Saint Louis Marie de Montfort said, "*in Scripture Mary was silent; but in the last days, she will be like John the Baptist, heralding the coming of Christ. She will no longer be silent.*" In this apparition, Mary said nothing, but she said everything. But we did not understand. In Fatima, she warned us, but gave us a way out - "*In the end, my Immaculate Heart will triumph.*" Too many people took that to mean we didn't have to move a muscle. Mary was going to take care of everything.

Now she is appearing all over the world and she is talking, warning, pleading. But this time, she's not talking about how she's going to do it, and how her Immaculate Heart will triumph. She's pointing to us. She's telling us to get up off our duffs, and get the job done. *Save the Eucharist; Save the Word; Save the Family; Save the World.* And she's not beyond sending Angels to teach us and direct us, as she did at Knock and Fatima. We really believe we're at zero hour. These may truly be the end times, the final days. Do we dare not listen and respond?

Angels and the Miraculous Medal

Paris is called the *City of Lights*. It is also called *Sin City*. One of the most sophisticated cities in the world, it is difficult imagining our Lady and Her Angels visiting here. Not only did they come, but Mary and her Angels chose one of the most fashionable districts of Paris, the Left Bank.

Streets are lined with tiny boutiques, tempting passersby to buy everything from chocolates to scarfs retailing for $150.00. Long a haven for artists, easels spill out onto the narrow streets of Paris as they attempt to capture on canvas, the magnificent Cathedral which juts majestically toward Heaven, as it dedicates itself and the city to the most elegant lady in Paris, or the world for that matter, Notre Dame de Paris, our Lady, my Mary.

As we dodge between cars busily trying to get somewhere first, and squeeze past push carts and their vendors hawking bargains we cannot live without, we come upon a giant department store called Bon Marché. But more importantly, we find sandwiched in between two of its annexes, on a side street, a small courtyard, at the end of which is a chapel.

From the street, all that can be seen is the address, 140 Rue du Bac, and a little plaque, hardly noticeable to the bustling shoppers trying to avoid the cars that race down the street at breakneck speed. The plaque shows both sides of the Miraculous Medal. The little sign underneath reads "*La Chapelle de la Medaille Miracleuse*". It's not difficult to recognize those who know where they are, as opposed to those who do not. The worshipers wear an expression of awe as they enter the courtyard, onto its hallowed ground.

The contrast from outside to inside is incredible. Outside is a jungle of humanity, embracing the world and all its lies and all its trappings. But, as you walk through the portals of this courtyard, *inside*, a peace and serenity blankets you. On the left wall, as you walk towards the chapel, sculptured reliefs graphically recall the life of St. Catherine Labouré and the miraculous gift given to her. Although this is all intriguing, you find yourself drawn to the end of the courtyard, because you know that's where it all began, 161 years ago.

Mary summons her Army of Angels

The area around Boulevard St. Germain looked much different in 1830. Paris was in an uproar. It had just come through one of the most devastating times in the history of France, the French Revolution. During this plague on humanity, the Church was one of the main targets for persecution. Churches were desecrated; sacrileges committed on their altars; in particular, Notre Dame of Paris. Priests and nuns were tortured, and exiled from the country at best, or killed at worst. The Revolution failed, as it had to, because it was so satanic. But the effects of Lucifer's hold on the country, temporary though it was, was devastating. The attitude of the government towards the Church remained demonic.

The Revolution was followed by the reign of Napoleon Bonaparte. While he reopened the churches, he also attacked *the* Church. He conquered Rome, was excommunicated, and placed the Pope under arrest. After Napoleon's reign ended in 1815, havoc broke out *again* in Paris; the Church went underground once more. By the year 1830, a new revolution was in the making.

We know our dear Lady was upset about how her priests and nuns, as well as the laity were being treated. She had always been so loving to her children. It was *she* whom Jesus allowed to intercede on our behalf. How could she bring her earthly family back to Jesus and His Church? She sent her Angels to earth in search of a suitable soul, a pure vessel, who would be worthy and willing to be filled.

Mary has never been known to back down from a battle. So here we find her beginning her strategy for the salvation of France in the steaming streets of the city which had been her greatest supporter, but had become her greatest enemy. Paris was no match for Mary and her Army of Angels. She began her battle for Paris here in a little chapel on the Rue du Bac.

†

At the beginning of 1830, Zoe Catherine Labouré entered the convent of the Sisters of Charity at 140 Rue du Bac, an address which would become famous, very shortly. She felt at home almost immediately, as she entered the grounds of the convent. Three days after she arrived, the body of their Founder, St. Vincent De Paul, which had been hidden during the French Revolution, was returned to Paris, in solemn procession, and installed a block away at Rue De Sevres, where it remains till today.

The summer of 1830 was unusually hot. The city of Paris was to know some relief from the suffocating heat. On Bastille Day, July 14, a great storm fell, which managed to reduce the festivities to local *drunkenness* in the bars. As the storm rescinded, a wave of clean, refreshing air followed, cooling off the steaming streets. The gentle breezes soothed the citizens as well as their homes for a few days. But by the 18th of July, the heat began mounting again. There was no sign of relief in sight. With the oppressive heat came a rumbling unrest among the people.

July 18, 1830 saw great activity at the Motherhouse of the Sisters of Charity on the Rue du Bac. The next day was the feast day of St. Vincent de Paul. Preparations had been made for weeks, for the festivities to be held on July 19. Catherine had worked hard during the day with the other sisters, to insure that the chapel and the convent would be spotlessly clean for the feast.

Before retiring, each sister was given a relic, a piece of St. Vincent de Paul's habit. Not satisfied to wear the relic, Catherine swallowed hers. That night, Catherine fell into a *deep*, well deserved sleep. She heard her name called. She awoke to the sound of a young child: *"Come to the Chapel. The Blessed Virgin is waiting for you."*

Catherine's first response, half out of shock, and half out of drowsiness was, *"But how can I go across the dormitory? I will be heard."*

The child replied, *"It's half-past eleven. Everyone is asleep. Come, I am waiting for you."*

As she rushed to get dressed, and catch up with the child, she became aware that he was an Angel. Had he said *The Blessed Virgin* was waiting for her? She was sure she was dreaming as she floated down the hall towards the chapel. All the lights were brightly lit. She couldn't believe that none of the other nuns had awakened.

She entered the chapel. It was all aglow; candles were flickering, burning brightly throughout the little church. She looked around the chapel. She was alone, except for the Angel. He led her to the foot of the altar, where she knelt. She prayed. She waited. All that had happened was registering in her brain. Was she really waiting for the Blessed Virgin? The little Angel had said Mother Mary would be there. Or had he? She looked towards him. He was breathtaking beautiful. He didn't pay any attention to her. His eyes sparkled with tears as he gazed upon the Blessed Sacrament. It was as if his adoration were cutting through the heavy doors of the Tabernacle to his Lord.

She heard a rustling sound, like someone walking in a silk dress. She turned in the direction of the sound. The Angel said, *"Here is the Blessed Virgin!"*

Left:
The Angel bringing St.
Catherine Labouré to the
Chapel

Below:
Chapel of the Miraculous
Medal in Paris, France

Catherine's heart pounded furiously. From out of nowhere, the most beautiful lady she had ever seen, appeared before her. Catherine caught her breath. She knew without asking, that this was the Mother of God. Catherine thought to herself, *this is how Mary would look. But she's so young, so exuberant.* The Lady sat in the director's chair, reserved for the priest during Mass. A wave of emotion swept over Catherine. She had to be close to our Lady. She fell to her knees at the foot of the altar, and embraced the knees of the exquisite visitor from Heaven.

Mary sat with Catherine for what seemed like an eternity. She gave her private secrets, many of which were revealed towards the end of Catherine's life, and others which have never been made known. Our Lady said to her,

"Our dear Lord loves you very much. He wishes to give you a mission. It will be the cause of much suffering to you, but you will overcome it, knowing that what you do is for the glory of God. You will be contradicted, but you will have the grace to bear it. Don't be afraid. You will see certain things. You must report them. You will be given the words through prayer."

"The times are evil. Misfortunes will fall upon France. The king will be overthrown. The entire world will be overcome by evils of all kinds, but.....

"But come to the foot of this altar. Here, great graces will be poured upon all those who ask for them with confidence and fervor. They will be bestowed upon the great and the small."

This was the most unusual and intimate apparition of our Lady's that we have ever researched. She allowed this child to sit at her knees, and put her hands in the lap that had held the Baby Jesus. Mary poured her heart out to this young girl. While talking about some of the outrages which were in store for France and the Church, Mary held back tears, but finally broke down and cried.

We are allowed to witness the humanity of Mary, the compassion, the love and concern she has for us. There's a helplessness about her that wrenches at the deepest part of our soul. This sympathetic mother, so good, so loving, cries at our viciousness towards each other. We have to wonder how she can still love us in our wickedness. Why do we always mistreat this all-loving human being, who concerns herself with our welfare so much? Why does she torture herself for us? She has never done anything wrong. She has never committed a sin. She watched her Son suffer and die a cruel and inhuman death for our sins. Hasn't she had enough? Why should she have to continue to suffer for us?

The primary message that first night to Catherine was that she would have to endure much suffering, but Mary would be with her. She could have confidence that she would be successful in her mission, even when all seemed hopeless, if she followed Mary's instructions. As quickly as the Lady had come, she faded away. Catherine was alone in the chapel, except for the *Angel.* He accompanied her back to her dormitory. Her attention focused on the Angel. Could this be Michael? She remembered reading that St. Michael accompanied Mary everywhere she went. Could he have taken on the form of a child? Catherine looked at him. He just kept walking with her, back to her room. When she returned to her bed, the Angel faded away, as our Lady had.

Catherine didn't sleep that night. She was too excited. She couldn't believe what had just happened to her. Her mind raced through the events of the evening. She heard the clock strike two. She had been with Mary for almost two hours. She repeated in her heart all the things the Lady had told her. *A Mission!* She was being honored with a special mission! But what was it? Mary didn't tell her. Catherine was not concerned; she knew that when the time was right, our Lady would let her know exactly what she wanted.

Some of Mary's predictions to Catherine began to occur within a week of the apparition. Riots broke out in the city. Dead bodies littered the streets. However, our Lady kept her promise that her *Angels* would protect the spiritual children of St. Vincent de Paul. No harm came to St. Catherine or the sisters of the Rue du Bac.

Our Lady appeared to Catherine again on Saturday, November 27, 1830. There was none of the intimacy, none of the special closeness they shared in July. Mary did not even look at Catherine during this apparition, nor did she speak to her directly. Catherine received the message through inner locution. Our Lady had a definite focus this time. She went directly to the heart of the matter.

Catherine was in the chapel for evening meditation. All the sisters of the community were there, also. It was quiet time. A reading had been given, and the sisters were now meditating about how this insight affected their lives. Catherine's reflections were interrupted by a familiar sound. It was the rustling of the silk dress of her Heavenly friend. Catherine thought her heart would burst. She immediately opened her eyes and looked in the direction of the sound. To the right of the altar stood our Lady, more resplendent than Catherine could remember. Mary stood on a globe, and held a golden ball at arm's length, as if she were offering it up to God, her eyes directed towards Heaven.

In an instant, brilliant lights radiated downward from her hands. Catherine could see that the lights came from rings Mary wore, three on each finger. They were of various sizes. Catherine noticed that rays did not shine forth from each ring. Mary explained,

"The ball which you see represents the whole world, especially France, and each person in particular. These rays symbolize the graces I shed upon those who ask for them. The gems from which rays do not fall are the graces for which souls forget to ask."

Catherine was in a state of ecstasy, completely swallowed up in the joy of the vision. The golden ball vanished from our Lady's hands. Her arms went down, hands pointing outward, in an attitude of welcoming. The rays focused themselves down to the globe on which our Lady stood. An oval frame formed around Mary, with the following words written on it,

Oh Mary conceived without sin
Pray for us who have recourse to you

Mary spoke to the heart of the young postulant again.

"Have a Medal struck after this model. All who wear it will receive great graces; they should wear it around the neck. Graces will abound for persons who wear it with confidence."

The image turned. Our Lady disappeared, to be replaced by a large **M**. A bar went through the **M**, from which extended a cross in the middle. Underneath the **M** were two hearts, one surrounded by thorns, symbolizing the Sacred Heart of Jesus, and one pierced by a knife, with droplets of blood dripping from it, symbolizing the Immaculate Heart of Mary. Twelve stars surrounded this image in the shape of an oval. *Slowly the image disappeared.*

St. Catherine Labouré never revealed her visitation from the Mother of God and the Angel to anyone but her confessor. She led an obscure life, serving old sailors who abused her verbally, every chance they had. And how did she live out her long life, no longer seeing Mother Mary, love being replaced by her patients' anger? I believe the Angel who brought her to Mary, never left her.

The visit by our Heavenly Mother and the Angel to St. Catherine Labouré set into motion a series of events which were felt immediately around the world, and to this day is a very strong part of our Marian devotion. There were many messages given the people of God, during this apparition.

The most important truth given to us was **The Immaculate Conception** *(Mary Conceived without Sin)*.

There was a great need for the doctrine of the Immaculate Conception of Mary to enter into the consciousness of the people. A radical heresy, Pantheism, had taken hold of most of Europe. *Pantheism claims that man is on a level with God, equal to Him. God is not a being, but is manifested in all the forces of the universe.* Originally, only the intelligentsia understood the heresy. But by 1830, it had sifted down to the common man.

Pantheism is a direct contradiction with the centuries old belief of Catholics regarding the Immaculate Conception of Mary. Our belief that only Jesus and Mary were born without sin, clashed with the new heresy of man being equal with God, which had caused confusion and division. There was a need to make the truth *clear* to the faithful.

Mary began her crusade for renewal of devotion to her Immaculate Conception on the Rue du Bac in Paris. She continued pressing the point home until Pope Pius IX, under the inspiration of the Holy Spirit, officially proclaimed the doctrine of the Immaculate Conception on December 8, 1854. In the event that there was still any doubts in the minds of the faithful, she appeared to St. Bernadette Soubirous at Lourdes in 1858, and said the words "**I Am the Immaculate Conception.**"

Sweet Mary has always loved us. She comes to us in times of trouble. She ignores the hostilities against her, but fights with her *Angels* by her side, like a tigress to protect her Son against attacks. The battle goes on, but she shows no signs of weakening. She's up to it. She's dug her heels into the earth, and promises not to give up on us, as long as there's still time, and even a handful of believers. We wonder, though, how many believers there are, and just how much time is left.

†

Alphonse Tobin Ratisbonne's Conversion

Through the work of Mary and the *Angels*, the Miraculous Medal, as it became known, spread its miracles all over the world. In the first ten years, Europe was blanketed with devotion to Mary and her new medal. It had almost become a common occurrence for miracles to happen when the *Angels* brought requests to our Lady under the auspices of the Miraculous Medal. There are those who believe the petitioner's faith was so strong, miracles were able to be accomplished. Others say the miracles gave people such faith in our Lady and the *Angels'* intercession, it was a foregone conclusion that miracles would come about, and they did! But Mary had some very definite ideas about who was going to do *what* in her war against Satan. One of those whom she had her eye on was a Jew, Alphonse Ratisbonne. No one was safe from Mary and her *Angels*.

Alphonse Ratisbonne was born into a very wealthy Jewish family. He was a lawyer and banker. Although Ratisbonne had many friends of different religions, including Protestants, he had a singular hatred for the Catholic Faith. His older brother Theodore's conversion to Catholicism, and resultant ordination to the Priesthood, smoldered an anger within Alphonse that extended to refusal to even speak to his brother. Their parents, although not pleased with their son Theodore's decision, nevertheless forgave him. The angry and resolute Alphonse *sat shiva*[1]. For him, his brother was dead! He had betrayed the Jewish Faith!

In 1841, Alphonse was preparing to marry a Jewish girl. He thought he might as well travel while he had the

---

[1]*sat shiva*-when a person dies, his family mourns for seven days; they do no labor of any kind, not cooking, not even shaving. In many of the extremely Orthodox Jewish families, when a child adopted Christ as their Messiah it was tantamount to dying in their eyes. To sit shiver for that *defector* was a sign of unforgiving, to the point of refusing to accept his or her existence any longer, in the family.

chance, before settling down. Although his plan was to visit Malta, Mary sent the *Angels* to block every move he made in that direction. He landed in Rome. He checked into a hotel and who should he run into, but his friend Gustave Bussière. Now, it just happened that Gustave's brother Baron Bussière had recently converted to Catholicism!

Alphonse went the normal tourist route; he hopped from the Colosseum, to the Roman ruins, to the Forum, and finally to St. Peter's. He hated Rome almost as much as he detested the Catholic Faith. But being well brought up, he felt he should pay a visit to his old friends before departing quickly for Naples and ultimately Malta.

When he arrived at his friend's home, Gustave was not there. Alphonse went to leave his card. The servant mistook this to mean, he wanted to be ushered into the presence of the Baron. There is nothing in this world more zealous than a convert, unless it is a recent one. Poor Alphonse was attacked by the Baron. He couldn't let him leave without learning the truth about the Catholic Faith. As the Baron evangelized, Alphonse threw back the persecution of the Jews in the Rome Ghetto, which of course, he blamed on the Church.

The Baron handed Alphonse a *Miraculous Medal.* Alphonse hit the roof; *this* was another one of those Roman superstitions that repulsed him. *"Well*," challenged the Baron, "*if it is a superstition, then you won't mind wearing it, as it can't affect you, negatively or positively.*" Alphonse allowed the Baron's little girl to place the medal around his neck. Not satisfied, the Baron further challenged Alphonse: "*Say the Memorare; after all if, as you say, this is all nonsense it can't do you any harm, can it?*" Ratisbonne agreed, reluctantly. "*Oh*," continued the Baron, "*I have only one copy, so would you copy the prayer and leave the original here?*" Was the Baron trying to buy time? He certainly could have gotten another copy of the Memorare. In any event, as Alphonse began to write down the prayer, *Angels* surrounded him. He felt a strange sensation. As he later said, "*It was like an aria from an opera which you sing without thinking, and then feel annoyed at yourself for singing it.*"

The Baron told a friend, Count de la Ferronnays, about Alphonse. The Count promised to pray for him. He later told his wife, he had gone to St. Mary Major[2] and had prayed twenty Memorares for Alphonse. That night, the count suffered a massive heart attack and died.

The Lord had all His *Angels* in place. On the evening of January the 19th, Alphonse had a *vision*. He saw a plain, bare cross. It disturbed him. He could not escape it. The next day, he set about making his final good-bys. He wanted to get out of Rome, and fast. He bumped into the Baron who was on his way to the church of S. Andrea delle Fratte to make final arrangements for his friend, the count's funeral. The Baron shared with Alphonse, how his friend had prayed for him. What could Alphonse do; he accompanied the Baron to the church. The Baron asked Alphonse to wait in his carriage, that he would try to do everything, quickly. But Alphonse insisted on coming into the church, to look around at the beautiful art collection.

As he was idling away the time, studying the exquisite architecture, suddenly *a huge black dog* came bounding from out of nowhere. He kept leaping in the air, dashing back and forth, blocking Alphonse from leaving. The dog frightened him, as he did not appear playful, but rather *threatening*. As quickly as he had appeared, the dog disappeared. As soon as he stopped shaking, Alphonse saw rays of light bursting forth from the *Guardian Angels'* chapel! They were like beacons on a lighthouse; only *he* was the ship who had lost his way and needed to come ashore.

---

[2]The first church built for Mother Mary in Rome. It is one of the major basilicas of Rome and is one of four churches, with a holy door, which is opened every twenty five years during the Holy Year.

He entered the *Guardian Angels'* chapel. There, before him was the most beautiful woman he had ever seen, the incomparable Mother of God, Mary Most Holy. He lifted his eyes to hers. He felt himself being drawn, almost hypnotized by those loving, peace-filled eyes. He felt he would fall into her eyes and be swallowed up. She was standing, her arms outstretched, just as she appeared on the Miraculous Medal. It was time for their long-awaited rendezvous. Our Lady didn't speak, but his heart *knew* and he was finished!

Like another Jew before him, St. Paul, he was blinded to everything but his new life in Jesus. The Lord had used His Mother to call Alphonse to His Church. Alphonse took instructions and was received into the Church. But that's not the end of the story. He was from a very prominent family, as was the Count who had prayed for him. The account of Ratisbonne's conversion spread all over Europe. The Lord used Alphonse Marie (the name he chose) Ratisbonne to make His Mother's Miraculous Medal well known. It had only been, up to this point, a very local gift. Now, through this conversion, the whole world would know and be consoled by the intervention of the Miraculous Medal.

Who was the black dog? Could he have been Il Grigio, the ferocious dog who was Don Bosco's protector?[3] *Why* did our Lady appear in the *Guardian Angel's* Chapel? Does anyone stand a chance against Mary and her Angels, when she decides to bring you to her Son, Jesus? *Is it time for your long-awaited rendezvous with Mary?*

---

[3]See chapter on Saints and Angels - *Don Bosco and Il Grigio*

Fatima and the Angel

The Angels are always with us. Take any important incident in the history of the Church, or the history of the world, and you will find Angels. When it's time to save humanity from itself and its aptitude for self-destruction, Jesus, Mary and legions of Angels descend upon the earth to get us out of the impossible situations we've created for ourselves. A perfect case in point is the Angels' activities at Fatima.

Portugal has always been a very special place in the hearts of our Lord Jesus and His Mother Mary. It has been consecrated to our Blessed Mother for many centuries.

In **Fatima**, in **1917**, she gave us the message of penance and prayer.

In **Batalha**, about twenty miles from Fatima, a promise was made to our Lady to build a great church in her honor if she would help the Portuguese people defend themselves against Spain. A *victorious* battle took place on the day before the *Feast of the Assumption* in **1385**.

In **Alcobaca**, in a cluster with Fatima and Batalha, there is a monastery which was built in thanksgiving to our Lady for enabling the Portuguese to recapture the city of Santarem from the Moors in **1152**.

Santarem, part of that cluster, is also the site of a Miracle of the Eucharist in **1225** or **1247**.[1]

World War I

Let us go back in time to the Spring of 1916. The world was in turmoil. A World War was devastating Europe. Bodies were strewn over the farmlands of France and Germany. The bitter winter had been hell, slowing troop movement to a virtual standstill. Because of the brutal weather, soldiers of both sides were pinned down in foxholes

---

[1]Covered in chapter on Santarem in "This is My Body, This is My Blood...Miracles of the Eucharist".

for months at a time; all in feeble attempts to control small patches of land. Mustard Gas, the Agent Orange of the early 20th Century, was ripping out the lungs of those who breathed it. Humanity had absolutely no regard for his brother and sister.

In Russia, a monster was being created which would cast its hideous, godless shadow over the entire world. The Bolsheviks were not involved in the World War. They were too busy destroying their own people, in purges that would parallel the outrages of Adolph Hitler and his gang of perverts some 20 years later.

The tiny country of Portugal was having its own problems, mostly financial. In the hundred years prior to this time, Portugal had lost most of its colonies in South America. They had only established a republic some 6 years before, which had not quite worked. No one knew how to run the government wisely, and so the country fell into chaos and disorder. In a very brave, but very unwise move in 1916, they declared war on Germany, and sent troops into France to fight the Huns. The effect of this on the homefront was disastrous.

The history of the country was filled with tales of kings making pledges and commitments to our Lord Jesus and our Lady, in exchange for favors received. The attitude of the new leaders of Portugal was just the opposite, not unlike those of other newly formed republics. They equated the Church with the Monarchy. Portugal had thrown the Monarchy out in 1910, and was now persecuting the church, in an attempt to throw it out of the country.

The one power they had not taken into consideration, in their harassment of the Church, was its Head, Jesus Christ, a faithful God to a sometimes unfaithful people. They had forgotten about the strength of His love, His patience, His adeptness at changing people's hearts, and His Mother, my Mary. They were so sure they could succeed without God, they ignored the Source of their well-being. They were children playing in the adult world, without knowing what they were doing. Fortunately, Jesus cannot resist caring for wayward children.

We can't help but wonder why our Heavenly Family bothers with us. We continue to make the same mistakes, commit the same outrages that began with the murder of Abel by Cain. Thank Jesus for His Mother Mary. She is so touchable. It's that one teardrop she sees falling from the eyes of a mother whose baby has been killed, whose husband has been dragged off, screaming into the night, never to be seen again. Those outrages against humanity, which have gone on since the dawn of creation, is that which propels her into action. We had great need of our Lady's help in 1916. There were no kings left in Portugal to plead the cause of the people. So, it was up to the mothers to pray to our Lady for peace. She heard those prayers, and answered them, as only she could.

Angel of Peace to the rescue.

A great plan was conceived in Heaven. It began to make itself known, in a very small way, to three little shepherds in the remote little farming village of Aljustrel, in the Spring of 1916. It was still early in the season, the rainy time, before the weather warmed up. That morning, Lucia dos Santos, and her cousins Jacinta and Francisco Marto, led the sheep to the Loca de Cabeco to graze. The ground and the grass were wet from the morning rain. They could feel the moisture on their feet, through their little sandals. Drizzle began to fall gently from the sky. The children ran up a hill to a cave where they could shelter themselves and their sheep until the rain stopped. They ate their lunch in the cave; and although the rain stopped, and the skies cleared, they stayed there, playing a game with pebbles.

The early afternoon was very calm, very still. The children became mesmerized by their game. Suddenly, a powerful blast of wind ripped through the trees, bending the branches as it whipped around the little cabeco, breaking the still of the day. The children snapped out of their daydreaming. They jumped up like a shot, looking around frantically to find out what was causing the abrupt change in weather. All at once, their eyes zeroed in on a bright light far off in the distance, approaching them, faster than the speed of light, so they thought. It drew closer to their little cave. As it moved closer, it became larger. They could make out the transparent figure of a person. Their hearts pounded. They were too frightened to speak. Closer and closer the vision came, until it was almost on top of them.

It was a beautiful young man. His long mane of blonde hair blew in the breeze. There was a sensitivity about him, almost contradicted by a forceful strength. His eyes were cobalt blue. When he looked at the children, they could feel his stare to the depths of their souls. While they were frightened of this majestic figure before them, they couldn't take their eyes off him. He spoke to them very gently, "*Do not be afraid. I am the Angel of Peace.*"

From this title by which the Angel called himself, we can be fairly certain it was the beloved of Mary, St. Michael the Archangel. Although the Angel never actually called himself by the name of the Prince of the Heavenly Hosts, Scripture and the Litany of St. Michael gives him the title, "Angel of Peace" among many other equally powerful honors. It has also been handed down in Church tradition and Marian devotion that wherever our Lady is, St. Michael is sure to be found close by.

The Angel continued, "*Pray with me.*" He prostrated himself on the ground, and said the following prayer.

"My God, I believe, I adore, I hope, and I love You. I ask forgiveness for those who do not believe, nor adore, nor hope, nor love You."

The children, in a state of shock, followed suit. They put their heads to the cold stone, and repeated what they heard the Angel say. He repeated the prayer three times. They did the same. Then he stood up again. He seemed to be nine feet tall. He looked at them. *"Pray in this way"* he told them. *"The Hearts of Jesus and Mary are ready to listen to you."* Then he took his leave. A gust of wind followed him as he turned into a bright light again, becoming smaller and fainter as he drew away from them. Finally, he was gone.

Silence! The sound of silence was so strong, it completely overpowered them. They looked at each other. No one said anything. They were dumbfounded. For the rest of the day, they thought of nothing else. They didn't play anymore. They stayed off by themselves, each separated from the other. Every now and then, they would look at one another. They were in shock. The three never considered telling anyone what had happened. It was too intimate. They quite honestly didn't even know how to describe it. There were no words.

The plan was in motion. Ponder in your hearts, for a moment, the words of the Angel. *"I ask forgiveness for those who do not believe, nor adore, nor hope, nor love You."* Who was he talking about? Was it the leaders of this country who had rejected our Lord Jesus in the Blessed Sacrament, His Mother Mary, and all things the people had always held dear? Were they trading Jesus in for something better, and if so, what? The words fit the pattern of what the official attitude of the country towards the Church had become. They certainly had stopped loving Jesus. Adoring Him was out of the question, and they seemed to have lost hope in the ability of their God to provide for His children. But whatever they had hoped to receive in return for their betrayal was not forthcoming. The government of Portugal continued to be extremely poor, up until the present time. Judas got 30 pieces of silver for his treachery. These wretches did not even get that.

Could it be that Mary was looking into the future, to that fateful day in January 1973, when the Supreme Court of the United States ruled in favor of Abortion, opening the door to wholesale murder in our country of yet unborn American Citizens, and future exploitation of the fetuses for Nazi-type experiments? The atrocities of the concentration camps appear like fairy tales, in comparison to the slaughter and ghoulish experimentation on unborn citizens of our "Free" society. Did she watch, in tears, as an entire generation of Americans was murdered by Abortion and Drug Abuse? Can she see into the 1990's, and the turn of the century, as the impact of that lost generation will be felt in our country?

The Angel returns

The second apparition of the Angel set the tone for what was to come a year later. We were in serious times. There was a great urgency for return to prayer, penance, sacrifice and mortification. It was the Summer of the same year, 1916. Portugal, and especially the Serra where the children lived, became unbearably hot. The flocks were brought out in the pre-dawn hours to graze while there was still a cool breeze in the air. Later, they would be kept out of the hot rays of the sun until evening, when the weather would cool off again, somewhat.

During this time Lucia and her cousins tended sheep in back of Lucia's house, near the well. It was here that the Angel came to them a second time. It was the lunch hour. All the sheep had been put away, to protect them from the hot sun. The children were sitting under some trees near the well. The Angel did not make an entrance, the way he had the first time. One moment, they were alone; the next, he was there. His manner was one of impatience.

"*What are you doing?*" he said. "*Pray! Pray! The hearts of Jesus and Mary have merciful designs for you. Offer your prayers and sacrifices to the Most High.*"

Lucia asked him "How are we to make sacrifices?"

The Angel responded "*In every way you can, offer a sacrifice to the Lord, in reparation for the sins by which He is offended and in supplication for sinners. Thus you will bring peace to our country. I am its Guardian Angel, the Angel of Portugal. Above all, accept and bear with patience the sufferings which the Lord will send you.*"

The Lord gave the children very important messages, through the Angel. For one thing, it was determined that they would be sacrificial lambs. They were required to suffer and do penance for the sins of many others. When the Angel asked them to "*above all, accept and bear with patience the sufferings which the Lord will send you,*" the message was reminiscent of that given to Bernadette at Lourdes, when our Lady told her "*I cannot promise you happiness in this world, but in the next.*"

In another part of his message to the children, he told them: "*In every way you can, offer a sacrifice to the Lord.... in supplication for sinners.*" We can't help thinking of "The Little Way" of St. Thérèse of Lisieux, the Little Flower. She never did anything spectacular in her entire life. When she died, nuns in her own community didn't know who she was. But in her life story, "Autobiography of a Soul," she tells us that everything she did, every little thing, she offered as a sacrifice to Jesus for the conversion of sinners.

It was after this second apparition by the Angel that we learn that Francisco had never heard the words of the Heavenly Visitor. As in the previous vision, the children were completely stunned by what had happened. They couldn't talk about it. Francisco had a burning desire to know what had been said. First he asked Lucia. She was not able to talk. She told him to wait until the next day, or ask his sister, Jacinta. Francisco went to his sister. She, too, was unable to put into words how the Lord had touched her in the deep recesses of her soul. She told him to wait until the next day.

The next day, Lucia told him what the Angel had said in both apparitions. He didn't understand all the big words that were used. Lucia explained their meaning as best she could. His tiny heart was filled with love of Jesus and the Angel. He thought of nothing but the Angel and his visit.

From that time on, the children prayed all the time. They found themselves shying away from the other children of the village. They had been just like the others before the Angel's apparition. Now, their entire beings were taken up with matters of the Spirit.

The Angel prostrated himself before the Eucharist

In the Autumn of 1916, the Angel of Peace, Saint Michael the Archangel, visited the children once more, in a most dramatic way. They were at the Loca de Cabeco again, caring for their sheep. Suddenly, he appeared above them, holding a Consecrated Host in one hand, and a Chalice in the other. Drops of Blood fell from the Host into the Chalice. He looked at them with an expression that was gentle, yet serious. This was a very important visit.

The Angel prostrated himself on the ground, leaving the Host and Chalice suspended in mid-air. He began to pray:

"Most Holy Trinity, Father, Son and Holy Ghost, I adore You profoundly and I offer You the most precious Body, Blood, Soul and Divinity of Jesus Christ, present in all the Tabernacles of the world, in reparation for the outrages, sacrileges, and indifference by which He is offended and by the infinite merits of His Most Sacred Heart and through

The Angel of Fatima with Lucia, Francisco, and Jacinta
"Take and drink the Body and Blood of Jesus Christ,
horribly outraged by ungrateful men.
Repair their crimes and console your God."

the Immaculate Heart of Mary, I beg the conversion of poor sinners."

He remained in the prostrate position for a time; then rising, he took the Host and Chalice into his hands. He gave the Host to the older of the three, Lucia, and the Blood of our Lord Jesus to Francisco and Jacinta.

As they drank from the Chalice, he said *"Take and drink the Body and Blood of Jesus Christ, horribly outraged by ungrateful men. Repair their crimes and console your God."*

After this, the Angel prostrated himself on the ground once more, and repeated the prayer he had said to the Trinity at the beginning of the Apparition. The children prostrated themselves, and prayed with him. Then the Angel rose, and looked at the children. They could feel a tingling inside of them. They were not sure if it was because of the unwavering stare of the Angel, or the burning of the Eucharist they had received inside their bodies.

After what seemed an eternity, but was actually a matter of seconds, the Angel slowly disappeared. The wind whistled through the Loca de Cabeco. It was beginning to get cold, but the children could not feel it. They were flushed by the Eucharist inside them and the Angel's presence. They stared for a long time into space. They could not speak.

We have to stop here again to try to understand the full impact of what the Angel was saying in his prayer, and what was really happening. We mentioned that in his first two apparitions, he prayed regarding *"those who do not believe, nor adore, nor hope, nor love You."* In this apparition, he used words such as *"outrages, sacrileges and indifference"*. The words were more intense. And yet these were *little people* he was speaking to. How could they be expected to understand what the Angel was saying to them? After all, Lucia was nine years old, Jacinta seven, and Francisco six years old. Look around you at your children of that age. Could you for a moment believe that they would be able to understand language of this magnitude?

There is no question that these were special children, hand-picked by our Lord and our Lady. The Angel's role was to prepare them for the task at hand. The Lord was angry. Mankind was on the verge of The Lord's Wrath. He had reached the proverbial "*Last Straw*" with us. Tribulation was on its way. The adults wouldn't listen to Him. Perhaps the children could get the message through to them. Does this sound at all like what's going on in our world, today? Are the events of the last few years a rerun of Fatima of 1916-1917? Is the Lord sending His Angels and His Mother to give us one more chance, before it's too late? Is it already too late? Have you seen any Angels lately?

Angels in Medjugorje?

(**Author's Note:**

"By their fruits, you shall know them." When Padre Pio was under fire from the Vatican in 1923, when everybody was warned to stay away from him, when he was ordered not to say Mass in public, or hear confessions, or perform any of his priestly duties, or show the wounds of his stigmata, a Bishop, Alberto Costa, wrote a plea for sanity with regard to Padre Pio.

He began with "*By their fruits, you shall know them.*" Then he continued, "*Innumerable souls return to God; reawakenings in the faith, change of habits, frequent reception of the Sacraments, especially on the part of men who had been away from them for many years...the impression which increased my desire to return to this house which is hallowed by the perfume of the exceptional virtue of the young religious.*" Does this sound familiar?

Padre Pio has been proven by the test of time. The Cause for his Beatification has been opened. We believe he will be honored by the Church within this century, which only gives us another nine years.

We are obedient to Mother Church in all things. Medjugorje has not yet passed the test of time. We are aware that there is a split as to opinions on Medjugorje, just as there was on Padre Pio. We are also aware that the final decision is not in yet from the Vatican on Medjugorje. We just ask that you not judge Padre Pio, or Medjugorje, or us, for that matter, for what we believe is happening there. Let the fruits and the Church be the determining factor.)

†

Wherever you find Mary, you're sure to find Angels. From the Annunciation onwards, Angels have always been constant companions during our Lady's visits to Planet Earth. We believe that the Archangel Gabriel played a very strong part in Mary's life from the day he announced to her the Good News that she would be the Mother of God, all through her pregnancy, including the messages he gave Joseph in a dream, and the flight into Egypt. We believe Gabriel was with Mary all her life, protecting her, consoling her. It is believed that Gabriel ministered to Jesus in the Garden of Gethsemane.

St. Michael the Archangel is said to be Mary's personal protector. When she goes into Purgatory to bring souls into Heaven, usually on Christmas Day, Michael accompanies her. She is the Queen of the Angels. The accounts of Mary and Angels have been a part of our belief from the very beginning. Angels heralded Mary in the Chapel of the Miraculous Medal in Paris, and came to the children in Fatima the year before she did.

So it would not be difficult to accept that if Mary is in Medjugorje, there will be Angels there, too. It makes a lot of sense. We just never thought about it until it was brought to our attention, first in a very gentle, loving way, by a precious soul, and then with a two-by-four, by the Lady herself, just to get our attention.

†

A friend from Baton Rouge told us about an experience she had with a *"beautiful young man"* on the road to Mt. Krizevac during her trip to Medjugorje. It had been a very cold morning, with dark clouds lurking in the sky, just waiting for an opportunity to dump buckets of rain on the unsuspecting pilgrims. So when our friend, Marguerite, her husband, and another couple began the long trip up the mountain, they were dressed for bear, equipped for anything and everything the weather might throw at them. The only thing they weren't prepared for was the sun to come out, and the day to become warm. This happened when they were about halfway up the mountain. They had to take off the heavy jackets they had been wearing, plus the scarves, gloves and hats.

There Marguerite was, loaded down with a sweater, a jacket, gloves, a hat and whatnot. She had gotten separated from the others who were now out of sight. She continued the hard trek, fighting the jagged rocks which could easily twist her ankle. She prayed the Rosary, which helped a little, but she was running out of breath and energy. Suddenly, she heard a noise behind her. She turned to see what she termed a *"beautiful young man"* with long blonde hair, and blue eyes, dressed in jeans, bounding up the mountain. He was tall and slim. He wasn't actually walking on the rocks, but leaping gracefully, like a gazelle, along the sides of the path.

He stopped in front of Marguerite, smiling at her. He was not even slightly out of breath. God bless the young. She looked up at him. The sun blinded her momentarily, placing the young man in a silhouette, with the sun forming a halo about his head. But she was then able to see through the brilliance. The young man had piercing cobalt blue eyes, and the most beautiful expression on his face. He spoke to her:

"Hi. You look like you could use some help."

She didn't understand what he meant. He pointed to all the baggage she was carrying.

"Can I help you carry some of that stuff up the mountain?"

Now, Marguerite is a very trusting person under most circumstances, and they *were* in Medjugorje, but still, she hesitated. Before she could say yes or no, the young man very gently gathered up all her baggage, and began to carry it up the path. She felt like she weighed about twenty pounds less. It must be all right, she thought. He seemed like such a nice young man.

They walked together for awhile. Marguerite couldn't help but notice the young man never walked on the path, but jumped from side to side, climbing just a little in front of her. The reason she was so aware of this, she told us, was because she had to keep looking up at him. Every now and then, he would stop and help her over a rough grade, but pretty much he was in front of her all the way. They talked a little, about Medjugorje, our Lady, the visionaries, and just the joy of being in this place. Marguerite did most of the talking. The young man listened, smiling, but he seemed to be silently praying the Rosary under his breath, as they walked.

Finally, he said to Marguerite, "*I'm going to go on ahead. I'll meet you a little farther up the mountain.*"

Marguerite didn't know what to say or do. All she could think of was to shout out, "*What's your name?*"

The young man looked back, smiled at her, and answered, "*Ralph*".

Marguerite became a little concerned. She didn't know the young man. He seemed honest enough. But suppose he wanted to steal her belongings? She began to worry for sure. Much as she had enjoyed the leisurely pace she had taken while he was with her, she found herself climbing for all she was worth, trying to get up the mountain as quickly as possible. She began praying doubletime, that the young man and her things would be there.

A very tired, worried, out of breath Marguerite finally got to the top of the mountain. But there, in a neat little pile, were all her belongings. She was so happy. She looked around for Ralph. He was nowhere to be seen. But her husband and the other couple were close by. They ran over to her. Her husband asked, "*How did your things get up here? They were here when we got here.*"

She blurted out, "*Ralph brought them up! Didn't you see him? He had to pass you on the way up.*"

She described the young man, and the incident. No one remembered seeing anyone like that pass them on the way up the mountain. But someone could have passed them, they thought, without their seeing him. They were praying and talking. They weren't paying attention to the people coming and going. Marguerite didn't say anymore, but she couldn't get the young man or the incident out of her mind. When we went to Baton Rouge to give a series of talks, about six months later, she had to tell us the story.

When Marguerite finished sharing with us, we smiled at her. *"Did you ever think,"* we asked her, *"that your Ralph might have been Raphael the Archangel, who is also the patron saint of travelers and safe journeys?"*

Her face lit up; she began to cry. *"Oh my Lord, Good Jesus, was that an Angel, was that the Archangel Raphael who helped me on the mountain?"*

The most natural answer we could give her was the most obvious, *"Why not?"*

Since that time, we have heard many stories of people experiencing unexplainable encounters with young men, who help them in some way and then disappear, or come from out of nowhere just at a time when they need help. But while we have never had a problem believing any of them, we never gave these incidents much thought, until Penny had her own experience in Medjugorje.

†

We brought a pilgrimage to Medjugorje for Passion Week, in 1988. And it was just that, *Passion.* Getting to Medjugorje has always been torment for us. It has never been an easy task. This year was to be no different. The airline bumped us from arriving in Dubrovnik, and left us stranded in Zagreb. Fifty of us were sitting around the airport, and no one seemed to care. Finally, I got my Sicilian up, and insisted the airline people assist us. At around 11 p.m., they finally gave us rooms in one of the worst hotels possible. The next morning, we got on a plane, and landed at Dubrovnik; then we began the bus ride to Medjugorje. Our housing was a mess. We were all over the village, which made it difficult for us to continue with the community spirit we had built up in the week we had been in Italy. I could feel my temperature rising, though it was freezing cold, and heavy rains were coming down.

We went to Mass at St. James that night, or rather tried to. It was right after our Lady had appeared in the choir loft, and the church was packed. We tried our hardest to work our way through the crowd. Bob was my bulldozer; but in half an hour of pushing, and being pushed, we never got beyond the vestibule. We tried to pay attention to the Mass, but suddenly I could feel myself being crushed on both sides. My ribs were breaking. I turned to Bob and said, "*I'm going to be ill. Please get me out of here.*"

If you think it's difficult trying to squeeze your way *into* St. James at one of these times, try getting *out*. It was near impossible. Bob pleaded in every language he could think of. "*The lady's sick! She's going to be ill! Clear the way!*" Nothing seemed to work. Dear Lord, get me out of here!

Finally, I could feel the cold air hitting my face. We were outside. After getting some breath, and feeling my stomach settle somewhat, I really got upset. I started complaining to Bob, "*This place is a carnival. There's no spirituality here. These people are acting like animals. I'm going to expose this place. Our Lady may have been appearing here once, but she's not here anymore. I'm going to tell the whole world that this place is a farce!*"

My husband is a saint. He can find humor in any situation. He said to me, "*Well, that will cut down the number of talks we have to give. No one will want to hear us anymore.*"

But I was on a roll. I answered, totally unappreciative of his brand of humor, for the occasion, and blurted out, "*I did not give up everything to lie. If Mother Mary is not appearing and I no longer believe she is, no matter what the cost I will tell any and everyone who will listen.*" I looked disgustedly at all the gypsies with pushcarts lining the main road in and out of the town. *"Look at that. Those people have nothing to do with our Lady. Even the garbage they're selling has nothing to do with our Lady. It's time someone told the poor deluded people who come here seeking their Mother!"*

This was pretty much my attitude that whole night and the next morning. It was Wednesday. We went to the 10:00 a.m. English Mass. It was to be the last English Mass until Easter Sunday. From then on, the only Masses would be the Croatian Masses at 7:00 p.m. The Church was packed, but we managed to get seats on the side. Fr. Pavich asked us to share our song books, as there were not enough to go around. There was a young man sitting on one of the benches, which ran up the side of the Church. He was facing our pew. He handed me his song book. I said to him, *"No, you keep it."* but he just smiled and gave it to me. I thought maybe he was a European, who didn't read English.

There was also a young man sitting next to me. A funny feeling went through me as I looked at him, but I couldn't figure out why. I had never seen him before. He was tall and handsome, with light brown hair.

When the singing began, I was in the middle; therefore, I held the book. Bob was on my right and the young man was on my left. I put my arm around the young man to draw him closer so he could see the song book. I cannot explain the feeling. I thought *Richard?*[1] Then, during the Lord's Prayer, we all held hands. When this young man took my hand, chills went through my body. *Richard?* I looked at his hand. It was impossible! Richard had heavy fingers like mine and my father's; this boy had long, slim fingers. Why did I feel this way? I tried to shake the feeling that my son was there. I couldn't let go of it it.

---

[1]Our son's name is Richard. He died in 1971, at age 19, of an overdose of drugs.

When it came to the Sign of Peace, the young man hugged me, as only my son and my grandson have hugged me. It was no polite, barely touching sign of Peace. This was the enveloping, consuming hug of someone I knew, who I loved and who loved me. I could feel tears welling up in my eyes. I had to know. I asked the young man, "What is your name?" I knew his answer before he spoke it. "*Richard!*"

I broke down completely. When I looked up, the other young man, the one who had given me the song book, was looking at me, with the most beautiful smile on his face.

When the Mass was over, I grabbed the young man, Richard. "*Where are you from?   How come you're in Medjugorje?*"

He was from Kansas. He said, "*I wasn't going to sit here near you. My group is on the other side of the Church. I wanted to be with them, but I found myself coming into this pew. It was as if our Lady was telling me to come over here, and then that guy told me to sit here.*" He pointed to the young man who had given me the song book. We both turned to look at him, but he was gone.

My heart was pounding; my head was reeling. I had to figure it out. I told Bob what had happened. He only smiled. He knew, but he couldn't tell me. I had to say it myself. Was it Richard? Did he come here to tell me something? Or was it Mary? Did she know the only way I would believe that she was truly here, was to bring out the big guns, my son Richard, to prove to me, to soften my hardened heart.

The next day, we boarded buses to go to Father Jozo's church for a talk. I still hadn't gotten the incident with the two young men out of my mind. I knew I believed. Mary had touched me. But I am a thick-headed Sicilian. I needed more. I wanted to see that young man, who had put Richard next to me. I wanted to find out who he was.

We were rushed off the bus, and everybody made a mad dash to get into the church, so we would get seats. I became completely occupied with that, when Bob grabbed me. *"You remember the young man who gave you the song book? He was outside, directing traffic. He smiled at you. Didn't you see him?"*

I left my husband and ran out, against the crowd. I had to find the young man. But now the parking lot was about empty. Only the drivers and some guides remained there. I looked inside the church; I couldn't recognize anyone. All I could see were thousands of heads. I just about found our group, but I spent the entire time we were in the church, looking for the young man. I never did find him. When we left the church, I tried in vain to find him. I was desperate. Our group kept yelling for me to get on the bus. Everyone was waiting for me. Finally, I got on the bus. He was nowhere to be seen.

Holy Saturday, Bob and I were scheduled to give a talk in the television room. The subject was to be, *"Where do we go from here?"* The room was jammed. We had to put young people on the floor, and line others up along the sides of the rows of chairs. There were others standing outside the door. I kept looking for either of the two young men, but I didn't see them. I wanted them to be there, because my subject was not necessarily the subject we had chosen to speak on.

I gave my own personal testimony. I shared how angry I had been, how I had said I hadn't believed Blessed Mother was here anymore, if she had ever been here. *And this is after having written a chapter in our book about our own personal miracles that had happened in Medjugorje.* Then I shared about this Passion Week, which had truly been passion for me. I shared how gentle our Lady had been with me, how she used the only person I would believe, my son, who is with her and our Lord Jesus in Heaven, to convince me that Mary reigns in Medjugorje. When it was over, a woman came up to me, put her arms around me and the two of us wept together. She thanked me for sharing my doubts; she said she felt guilty about the depression she had experienced, but now she was at peace.

As we left the talk, there was a big crowd on the road. They were heading in the direction of Mount Krizevac. In this huge crowd, one face stood out for me. It was him, the young man who had given us the songbook. I ran over to him. He smiled at me. He said, "*I hear you found your Richard.*"

Tears were streaming down my face. I had to know. "*What is your name?*" I asked him. He looked at me very gently. His eyes consumed me completely. He spoke very softly; he said one word, "*Michael*".

Our Lady did everything she felt necessary to get me back on the track. She used my son Richard, and my favorite Angel, the Prince of the Heavenly Hosts, Michael. And she did it all in Medjugorje.

Are there Angels abounding in Medjugorje? You bet there are. Are they there waiting for you? We believe they are. But they are not just in Medjugorje. They're in California, and Louisiana, and Arkansas. They're all over the world, and they're there for you and me. *I needed the Angels in Medjugorje!* I needed that sign. The greatest feat the evil one could have accomplished would have been to get me to stop believing in the work our Lady is doing in Medjugorje. She knows, I believe in the power of the Angels, in their desires to help us through this pilgrimage of life.

It drives me wild how I'm such a doubting Thomas. A beautiful priest once called me "*a doubting Thomasita*". I have no problem telling the whole world of the power of Jesus, the power of Mary, and the power of the Angels. I have no problem believing that God has given the Angels unique gifts for our welfare, or that they will use those abilities if only we ask them. But for some strange reason, it's so hard for me to believe it can happen to me. I'm as bad as the rest of you. I know I'm not worthy, and I believe that their love for me depends in some way on my own worthiness. That's not true at all. God and Mary and the Angels love us because they love us. They are love. They are there waiting for us to just say the word.

Don't be afraid to ask your Angel for help. He probably won't come to you dressed in battle gear, with sword drawn and red cape flying, like Michael usually does. He may not even look like an Angel. He may look like a young man with light hair and cobalt blue eyes, but is he really your Angel? Why not?

Saints and the Angels

Our Lord ascended into Heaven; and His followers, filled with the Holy Spirit, set out to spread His Word of hope to the people of God. But you can understand, then as now, the *enemy* Lucifer, leader of all the fallen angels, has never wanted this Good News to be heard; his plan, from the time of Genesis, has been to rob us of relationship with our Creator.

But we say, in times of crisis, whether in the world or in the Church, God always raises up Saints. Cardinal Newman said of the Saints: They *"rise up from time to time in the Catholic Church like Angels in disguise and shed around them a light as they walk on their way Heavenward."*

We would like to bring you only a few of the many occasions where Angels have played an important role in the lives of the Saints.

Let us begin with St. Stephen. (?-34 A.D.)

He was brought before the Sanhedrin. Some Jews from Cyrene, Alexandria, Cilicia and Asia convinced men to falsely accuse St. Stephen of blaspheming against Moses and God. His accusers heaped one lie upon another as they testified,

"This man never stops making statements against the holy place and the law. We have heard him claim that Jesus the Nazorean will destroy this place and change the customs which Moses handed down to us."(Acts 6:13)

All those who sat on the Sanhedrin stared at Stephen. He knew his fate, if he did not deny our Lord Jesus Christ. He could not have been looking forward to the painful death they had planned for him. Instead of fear or anger, all who sat on the council said *"his face was like the face of an Angel."* Was the Angel, who had consoled our Lord in the Garden, with him? Was St. Stephen reflecting the joy and peace of *His* Angel beside him?

St. Stephen stood before the Council. He brilliantly traced how unfaithful a people they had been from the time of Abraham to that very day. He powerfully concluded his debate with these words of condemnation,

> *"You stiff-necked people, uncircumcised in heart and ears, you are always opposing the Holy Spirit just as your fathers did before you.*
>
> *"Was there ever any prophet whom your fathers did not persecute? In their day, they put to death those who foretold the coming of the Just One; now you in turn have become His betrayers and murderers.*
>
> *"You who have received the law through the ministry of the Angels, have not observed it."* (Acts 7:51)

"The ministry of the Angels!" They had been given the law through the ministry of the *Angels!* And they dared not to follow it! His words brought about a fury that would not contain itself. Stephen did not look at the anger, at the threat to his life. As the members of the Sanhedrin gnashed their teeth, St. Stephen looked up to *Heaven* and cried out that he saw *"the Son of Man standing at God's Right Hand."* (Acts 7:56)

Did an Angel pull back the curtain between Heaven and earth so that Stephen could see beyond? Was an Angel reminding him of the Lord's promise never to leave him? Did an Angel echo the words of our Savior, *"Be not afraid. I go before you, always."*

Later, what or *who* gave St. Stephen the strength to ask the Lord to forgive those who were stoning him?

> *"As Stephen was being stoned he could be heard praying, 'Lord Jesus receive my spirit.' He fell to his knees and cried out in a loud voice, 'Lord, do not hold this sin against them.' And with that he died."*
> *(Acts 7:59-60)*

Forgive them for they know not what they do! Was the same *Angel* there with him that cried at the Crucifixion of our Lord Jesus? They are stoning Stephen to death, and he is not thinking of himself but of their immortal souls. When we speak here of the Angels being there to console him, when we suggest that they were there providing him with the greatest love a person can have for another, the unconditional love for his persecutor, we are not belittling this act of Stephen. Although the act, and the man who performed the act was filled with the Holy Spirit and gifted with power from above, Stephen was *human*. He had to choose, over and over again, to say *yes* to that Messenger from the Lord by his side, his Guardian Angel. The man Stephen was an *ordinary* man; but he was able to perform an *extraordinary* act that would live on after him, touching and transforming men's hearts for centuries to come. Was he alone? I think not. But he had no greater friend and companion than you and I have.

St. Peter in Chains (?-64 A.D.)

We continue with the New Testament. We find *Peter* in prison...*chained*! Scripture tells us that his community was praying to God for his safe release. *Praying*! And how did God respond? He sent *an Angel* to Peter. It was the night before Peter was to be condemned to die. He was sound asleep, chained between two guards. By the exit, stood other soldiers guarding it against his escape.

This troublemaker who was telling the people they were not slaves, but that this Jesus had made them free, had to be done away with. But God had another plan. Besides, those Christians praying for Peter would not let him alone. It is not known whether God sent one of His other Angels or used Peter's own Guardian Angel to free him. But the fact remains, we read that the *Angel of the Lord* put the two soldiers, on either side of Peter, to sleep, and then

"Suddenly an Angel of the Lord stood nearby and light shone in the cell. He tapped Peter on the side and woke him, 'Hurry, get up!' he said. With that the chains dropped from Peter's wrists. The Angel said, 'Put on your belt and your sandals!' This he did. Then the Angel told him, 'Now put on your cloak and follow me.'"

proceeded to do the same to those at the doorway. The Angel released Peter from his chains, commanded him to dress hurriedly, and then to follow him.

Now, put yourself in Peter's place. He thought he was dreaming. But he followed the Angel's prompting! The prison doors opened as the Angel and Peter approached. When they reached the courtyard, the iron gates flung wide. Before he knew what was happening, Peter and the Angel were proceeding down a dark and lonely street. When Peter turned to the Angel, to thank him, there was no one there. Only then, did he realize what had happened and *who* the Lord had sent to free him.

Peter went to where the disciples were staying. He knocked on the door. Rhoda, the maid, came to answer his knock. When she recognized Peter's voice, she was so happy that he was free, instead of opening the door, she ran to the disciples and told them Peter was at the door. Of course, their response was that she was mad! Even as she *insisted* it was Peter, they said it must be his *Angel*.

They reasoned, since it was humanly impossible for Peter to be there, it had to be his *Angel*, his Guardian Angel, who must have taken on his voice. When Peter persisted at his knocking, which now had grown into pounding, they finally opened the door. Upon recognizing him, they warmly embraced him and helped him into the house.

An Angel of the Lord comes to St. Paul (5-68 A.D.)

Paul was in prison, in Caesarea. Festus, the former governor of Caesarea, left for Jerusalem. He had kept St. Paul in prison for over two years, in an attempt to placate the Jews. When Festus arrived there, the Jews in Jerusalem tried to convince him to have Paul sent there from Caesarea, so they could kill him on his way. Festus, believing it only fair and just, that a prisoner be allowed to face his accusers, told the Jews to travel to *Caesarea* with him and accuse Paul in a court of law.

Festus and the Jews travelled to Caesarea. Paul was hailed into court. The Jews accused, and St. Paul very ably defended himself. Festus, trying to gain favor with the Jews, asked Paul, *"Would you be willing to go to Jerusalem and be tried on these charges before me there?"* Paul exercised his right as a Roman citizen, that he be tried by the Emperor.

Festus was in a quandary. What charges could he bring against Paul to the Emperor. The accusations, the Jews had made in Jerusalem, they did not make in Caesarea. King Agrippa and his wife came to Caesarea. Festus asked the King to hear the case against St. Paul. After hearing St. Paul, the King found no reason to keep St. Paul in prison, no less release him to the Jews. He said, "This man could have been released if he had not appealed to the Emperor."

It was decided, Paul and some other prisoners would travel to Rome. Out at sea, the ocean and the winds became so turbulent, Paul warned, it was too dangerous to go on. He prophesied, *"...there will be great damage to the cargo and to the ship and loss of life as well."* But the captain of the ship made the decision to go on. They stayed as close to shore, as possible. At first, they were encouraged by the soft wind that was blowing; but it soon turned into a roaring storm that was impossible to head into. So, they decided to travel with the wind at their back. The men then became afraid, the raging *northeaster* would carry them out to sea. If they were too close to shore, they would run into the sandbanks. It seemed there was no way out. In a frantic attempt to keep the ship from going down, they started to desperately throw provisions overboard. This was followed by the ship's equipment. Finally, they gave up all hope!

They had gone a long time without food. St. Paul stood before them and spoke,

"Men, you should have listened to me and not have sailed from Crete; then we would have avoided all this damage and loss. But now I beg you, take courage! Not one of you will lose his life; only the ship will be lost. For last night an Angel of the God to Whom I belong and Whom I worship came to me and said, 'Don't be afraid, Paul! You must stand before the Emperor. And God in His goodness to you has spared the lives of those who are sailing with you.' So take courage, men! For I trust in God that it will be just as I was told."

St. Paul had brilliantly debated and was able to save his life many times, when the Jews persisted in their attempts to have him executed. But on the ship, as he travelled to Rome, all his brilliant rhetoric and logic and persuasiveness could not change the minds of the men to remain in the harbor, and they all almost perished at sea. It was only when he spoke the message of an *Angel* of *God* that he was able to bring hope to men with no hope, aboard the ship. Was it that he spoke, now, not with his authority; but by quoting the Angel of the God Whom he adored and trusted, they could feel the power of *God* speaking through him!

It's interesting, isn't it. St. Paul knew and believed in the Angel of God. He trusted in his God, in His Love, in His Word that He would never leave him an orphan and that whatever he would face, *he and his Lord* would face it together. And the Lord came through!

St. Augustine and the Holy Trinity (354-430)

It is only fitting we write of St. Augustine and the Angels, after St. Paul. For, you see, it was the writings of St. Paul which most influenced St. Augustine to come home, at last, to Mother Church.

With all his education, with his never ending search for God, his unquenchable thirst for knowledge and

*St. Augustine sees a little boy, taking water in a shell from the
sea, trying to empty it. He asks the boy what he is trying to do.
The little boy tells him, "It is easier for me to empty the sea
with this seashell than for you to understand
the Holy Trinity."*

understanding, it is interesting that the answer to one of his most profound questions would come from a vision of a child or was it an *Angel*?

St. Augustine was walking by the seashore, one day meditating on the mystery of the Trinity. He came upon a little boy taking water from the sea, in a little shell. St. Augustine watched as the little boy scooped up some of the vast sea and then plunged the tiny shell back in, to extract more of the water. After awhile he asked the little boy what he was trying to do. The little boy responded he was trying to empty the sea with the seashell. We can just see St. Augustine smiling as he shook his head gently from side to side. *"You cannot empty the vast sea with that little shell. It is impossible."* The little boy, not in the least flustered, replied, *"It is easier for me to empty the sea with this seashell than for you to understand the Holy Trinity."* With that, the little boy disappeared.

Was our Lord sending His Messenger down to Augustine to tell him not to bother trying to figure out God, but to believe and live the belief that He passed on to the Apostles before him?

Saint Patrick and the Angels (418 - 493)

There has been an ongoing battle between Penny and Bob as to the origins of St. Patrick. He is the Patron Saint of the Irish, having evangelized the Emerald Isle in the middle of the Fifth Century. He is actually called *"The Apostle of Ireland"*. *But he was not Irish!* He had been kidnapped by Irish barbarians from the south of Wales as a teenager, and was brought to Ireland as a slave. So he had to be from somewhere else. His father is said to have been a Roman magistrate, and the family was Christian. So they probably were not British or Welsh. There's even a *slim* possibility that he was Italian. Sweet mother Mary, that would mean that Penny was right.

But we have an Irish Monsignor pastor from Tipperary, who insists St. Patrick was not Italian. So the choice is yours; believe Penny or Monsignor Tom. I would just like to leave you with this. I know I read somewhere that if you dispute the solemn words of an Irish priest, or better yet, an Irish Monsignor, especially when it comes to St. Patrick, there may be extra time in Purgatory for you. I'm not saying that's a fact for sure, but would you want to take that chance?

St. Patrick comes from a strong Christian heritage, especially considering the time in which he lived. He was born, most people believe, in the year 418. The Church had only been made legitimate by Constantine the Great, a century before. Patrick's father was a deacon, and it's believed his grandfather was a *priest*. This was before the laws of celibacy were instituted in the Church. He claimed a Roman background. It is also claimed his name was Patricius Magonus Sucatus. So the argument in favor of Italian heritage really does become very strong here.

His father was stationed in Wales when Patrick was kidnapped. Patrick was a slave in the northeast section of Ireland from age sixteen to twenty two. We're told he didn't know the Lord when he was kidnapped, even though his family was very religious. However, during his captivity, and six years of slavery, the Angels began working on him. Through their ministry, speaking softly to him, giving him moral support when the situation with his captors became extremely dangerous, he developed a strong faith in God, and committed his life to the Lord's Will. At the beginning, he didn't actually see the Angels; he heard them. They advised him; they taught him; they consoled him. After a period of time, he began to look forward to the time when they would come to him. He was very lonely without their companionship. Without them, he was really all alone.

By age 22, he was trusted more by his captors. He was not really treated any better, and the chores he had to perform were no better than when he was younger. But *now* he was given the job of keeping the watch. They were on the coastline of Antrim, on the northeast part of the country. Patrick was to watch for enemy ships at sea. One night, he fell asleep. An Angel spoke to him in a dream. He said to him, "*You have fasted well and soon will go to your own country.*" Patrick knew in his heart this was an Angel speaking to him, and so he waited.

Shortly thereafter, in a dream, the same Angel gave him a way to get out of the country. He had to make a two hundred mile trip to the coast on foot. That was the least of it. The voyage home was perilous. Although the journey was treacherous, and there were times when Patrick wasn't sure he would survive, the Angels performed *miracles*, and Patrick returned to his family, after six years of captivity.

Nothing is known for sure about the next twenty years of Patrick's life, other than he studied Theology to a great extent, was ordained, and listened again to the calling of the Angels. He constantly dreamt of Ireland. Though his parents pleaded with him not to return, his heart was helplessly lost in Ireland. When the Angelic visions began to *actually bring him letters,* he knew he could not ignore their contents, not even for his parents he so loved. In one letter, he read the words, "*The Voice of the Irish.*" The Angels whispered softly in his ears, "*We entreat thee, holy youth, to come and walk once more among us.*"

Needless to say, Patrick went to Ireland, and in a period of thirty years, from age forty to about seventy, he converted the entire country. It is said that at a given point in time, he converted *hundreds of thousands.* Now how could one person do that all by himself? He had to have help from the Angels. The Angels were very active in his ministry. As a matter of fact, he *wheeled and dealed* with the Angels. He spent an entire Lent one year at Croagh Patrick, which is a cone-shaped island on the western part of the country, in

County Mayo, actually not that far from Knock[1]. Remember we talked about *holy clusters*[2]? This could very well be an area of holy clusters.

At any rate, during this particular Lent, an Angel came to Croagh Patrick to have a conference with the Apostle of the Irish. Patrick asked for certain concessions for his people, for example; (1) the Irish would hold fast to the Faith until the end of time; (2) a tidal wave would cover the country seven years before the Final Judgment, so the Irish wouldn't be alive to witness this terrible scene; (3) every Irishman, doing penance, would not be doomed to hell on Judgment Day.

He seemed to do all right with these requests. But, as he laid down his demands, he may have gotten a bit carried away with himself. His last request, that he, Patrick, should be allowed to judge the people of Ireland on the last day, was more than the Angel could allow without a meeting on high. Patrick insisted he would not leave the mountain until he was granted that request. The story goes that the Angel left Patrick praying and fasting, while he made a quick round trip to Heaven, to confer with the Lord.

After much debate, and a review of Patrick's zeal for the Lord, plus all the work he had done, and would continue to do, it was determined that he would indeed be granted his desire to judge all the men of Ireland, on the last day.[3]

Patrick had a very special relationship with the Angels, all his life. Verification of this fact may come from a prayer which we were given at the cave of St. Michael in the Gargano. It goes like this;

---

[1]Knock: where our Lady appeared August 21, 1879 (you can read about it in the chapter in this book, Mary and the Angels at Knock and in *The Many Faces of Mary, a love story* by Bob and Penny Lord).
[2]See chapter on St. Michael and the Cave of Gargano
[3]according to Irish legend passed down over the centuries to this day.

"Dear Lord Jesus, we ask you to send all the Guardian Angels to form a protective circle around this (car, plane, boat), with St. Michael the Archangel in charge. St. Michael in front of us; St. Michael in back of us; St. Michael to the left of us; St. Michael to the right of us; St. Michael above us; St. Michael below us. (Keep anything that would harm us physically, spiritually, emotionally or mentally away from us, and bring us to our final destination to glorify Your Name.[4])"

We use that prayer all the time, and have for years, when we're doing any kind of traveling. But on researching this book, we found, in the chapter on St. Patrick, a prayer he had written, called *Lorica*, which he and his band of disciples prayed on the day the first major conversion in Ireland came about through his intervention. The last verse of the prayer goes like this,

"Christ with me; Christ before me; Christ behind me; Christ in me; Christ beneath me; Christ above me; Christ on my right hand; Christ on my left;...."

St. Patrick wrote that prayer somewhere around 460 A.D. St. Michael claimed the cave of the Gargano in the year 490 A.D. We're not suggesting that Patrick gave this prayer to Michael, or vice versa, but Patrick was very close to the Angels, and we would have to assume he was close to the Prince of the Angels, Michael. It would not be past the Angels or the great Archangel to pass on the same message to the Bishop in the Gargano as he passed on to Patrick in Ireland. We know that the Lord, in Scripture, often came in the guise of an Angel, so why not a prayer to either Jesus or His Angel?

Throughout Patrick's thirty year mission among the Irish people, he is known to have been helped *often* by his Angelic relatives. Even his last chore on earth, that of dying,

---

[4]This part we added ourselves

was dictated to him by the Angels. Patrick was aware the end was near. He wanted to return to his beloved Armagh to die there. To this end, he set out with great haste. He was stopped along the road, before he had made a day's journey. An Angel came to him, and told him to return to Saul, where he had built his first church, and made his first converts. It's possible that Patrick might have gotten his Irish up on this one, because after thirty years on this soil, he had taken on the personality of his people. However, the Lord was firm on this point, and Patrick returned to Saul to die on March 17, 493. Though we have nothing but our intuition to back up our convictions, it is our solemn belief that an Honor Guard of Angels appeared at his death, and carried their faithful brother up to Heaven with them. Sure and begorra, it must have been a grand sight to see.

Saint Francis of Assisi receives the Stigmata

Francis and three of his faithful companions, Friars Masseo, Angelo and Leo, went to the mountain of Alverna (La Verna) to pray, from the Feast of the Assumption (August 15) to the Feast of St. Michael (September 29). He called this period the Lent of St. Michael. Francis had a special rapport with Mary and Michael from the early days of his conversion. He went to them often, for comfort and consolation, when things got rough. He was going there now to *give*, by fasting in honor of their feasts; but he knew he would be *receiving* from them as well.

He always had an exalted devotion to St. Michael. He felt that Michael should be honored because he had the office of presenting souls to God. Francis also said *"Everyone should offer to God, to honor so great a prince (Michael), some praise or some special gift."* He loved Mary reverently. As he loved Jesus, he could not do otherwise than love *"the womb that bore Him."* He sang to her, offered special prayers to her, shared his joys and sorrows with her. She was his very best friend, the Mother of his God and Queen of all the Heavenly Angels. While he was honoring Michael on this mountain top, he was also honoring Mary on the Feast of her Assumption into Heaven, August 15, and her birthday, September 8.

There was a crag on that mountain, a deep crevice which separated one part of that high place from the other. Tradition has it that at the very moment Our Dear Lord Jesus died, this mountain split in two, as the whole earth shook violently, in protest over the demonic act of murdering our Savior. Francis loved to sit on that jagged rock, and meditate on the Passion of Jesus. The brothers brought him some bread and water from time to time, but for the most part, he was alone with his Lord and Savior.

According to the Divine Plan, another special Feast fell during the Lent of St. Michael. It took place on September 14, and was called The Exaltation of the Cross. Today, we celebrate it on the same day, but we call it the Triumph of the Cross. On that day, in 1224, the Lord gave Francis a distinctive gift, as reward for a lifetime of service. For on this day, Jesus gave His brother Francis, the gift of His wounds, His Stigmata.

Francis had been meditating deeply on the Passion of our Lord. He had asked his best Friend, Jesus, for two gifts. The first was that somehow, before he died, he might feel the wounds of Jesus in his own body and soul; and secondly, he might experience Jesus' love for those who inflicted the wounds on His Body, and killed Him. Francis went through *a dark night of the soul.* His mind kept interfering with his spirit. He struggled with what he had given up, his Fraternity, his Rule. He tried desperately to put these things in the back of his consciousness, and just zero in on the pains of His Redeemer. His humanity fought him all through the night, but with the dawn, a stillness, a heavy blanket of peace came over the mountain. Everything was quiet; not a sound from any of the creatures. It was as if they knew what was to come, and were preparing themselves for the entrance of a Heavenly Being.

Light began to emerge from the darkness. Francis thought it was Brother Sun greeting him. But the light was too intense, much stronger than the sun. The curtain separating Heaven from earth split open. A figure came forth, slowly, and carried the brilliant light with it. Francis couldn't look at it; the light was too strong. Then the Lord allowed Francis' eyes to open. Before him, suspended in the air, was a huge *Angel*, who appeared to be made of fire, he was so bright; but there were no flames coming from him. *He had six wings, two extended over his head, two extended as if for flight, and two covering his body.*[5] The angel was nailed to

---

[5]Celano First Life no. 94

a cross; the wounds of Jesus flared up, and shivered against the light. They were of a deep crimson, sprinkled with gold.

Francis stood up joyfully, to greet the Seraph[6]. At that moment, beams of heated illumination shot out of the Angel's wounds, and penetrated Francis' body, hands, feet and side. He fell from the force of the thrust; his body experienced devastating pain, mixed with inconceivable joy. His blood raced throughout his body; he was sure he would die. Then the sensation calmed down to a constant throb of joy and pain. He looked up at the Heavenly Creature. The eyes of the Angel were studying Francis. The stare was compelling. There was at once fear and bliss, mixed together. Francis didn't know what was happening to him. The eyes of the Angel were the most beautiful he had ever seen. He could not look away from them.

The Heavenly vision spoke gently to Francis' heart. He told him things he had to hear, which were for him alone; he would not in his lifetime, reveal them to anyone. He stayed with Francis for the better part of an hour. This is according to the testimony of the farmers, and mule keepers at the foot of the mountain. They mistook the brilliant light for the sun coming up, and began their day. Then, when it disappeared, and the natural sun came out, it was colorless by comparison.

Many insights were revealed to Francis on top of Mount Alverna. His whole life was put into perspective. He finally understood his journey, and while his humanity would tend to kick in over the next two years, he could always fall back on this time, and the revelations he received, and a peace would come over him.[7]

---

[6]Seraph is the name of the Angels of the Angelic choir of Seraphim, which is one of the choirs who adore before the throne of God. The word comes from the Hebrew "fiery" (Is 6: 1-4).

[7]Insert taken from "*Saints and other Powerful Men in the Church*"

*The Angels whisked St. Clare to the
Bethlehem of 1200 years before*

Saint Clare of Assisi (1193-1253)

We would like to share one of Clare's experiences, which is recounted in the *Fioretti*, the Little Flowers of St. Clare. It is the foundation for the title she shares with the Archangel Gabriel, *Patron Saint of the Airwaves*. It took place on Christmas Eve, 1252, the year before she died.

Clare was too ill to go to Midnight Mass services with her Sisters. She was too feeble to get out of bed. She lay there, her heart breaking, as she was to be deprived of our Lord Jesus in the Eucharist, on this special night. Her thoughts brought her back to the time in Gubbio, when Francis made the first Nativity Scene (after which all Nativity scenes in the future would be fashioned). Christmas had always been a joyous time for both Clare and Francis. She missed not having him with her on earth, but especially at this, so important a time.

She looked about the bare room that served as the sleeping quarters for the Sisters. Suddenly, there was a great light in the room. She could hear the sounds of Christmas hymns being sung at the great Basilica of St. Francis, in Assisi, barely a mile away. She felt herself being lifted out of her bed by the Angels. The cool breeze of the December night brushed across her face; she was transported to the church amidst what sounded, to her, like the voices of Angels. She could smell the sweet fragrance of burning candles, and altar incense. *She was taking part in the Midnight Mass at the Basilica.*

Then the Angels whisked her off to the east, to the Bethlehem of 1200 years before. She was brought down to the cave where the Infant Jesus was born. St. Joseph and Mary were there, in the company of the animals whose cave the Holy Family shared. *Our Lord Jesus came to her as a grown man, and placed the Sacred Host in her mouth.* Then she was transported back to the convent of San Damiano in Assisi. When her daughters in Christ came back upstairs from the Church, their joy was overshadowed by the great sorrow they felt because their Mother had missed the beautiful service. She smiled. Her face was flushed, but not from the illness. She told them of her experience, and how the Lord Himself had given her Communion. They sat by her bed listening and smiling. As they all fell off into a peaceful Christmas slumber, the soft, distant sound of Angels singing Gloria in Excelsis Deo could be heard.

St. Thomas Aquinas - the Angel of the Schools (1225-1274)

St. Thomas Aquinas, Doctor of the Church, is probably best known for his *Summa Theologica*[8]. As we wrote our book *This is My Body, This is My Blood...Miracles of the Eucharist*, we became close to St. Thomas Aquinas because of his great love and defense of the Holy Eucharist.

---

[8]Summa Theologica-the fullest exposition of theological teaching ever given to the world. (Butler's Lives of the Saints)

Thomas Aquinas came from a family of royal lineage, who had very definite ideas for their son Thomas' future. When he chose to enter the Dominican Order, it was not that they objected to him becoming a Priest; they had *plans* he would someday be a Benedictine. But not only a Benedictine, but Abbot of one of the holiest Shrines - the Benedictine Shrine of Monte Cassino.

His mother left for Naples to bring her son home and to his senses. When she arrived there, he was gone. The Dominican Friars had moved him to the convent of San Sabina in Rome. Not one to be easily discouraged, she immediately set out for Rome. When his mother arrived in Rome, Thomas was no longer there, having left for Bologna, Italy. Refusing to leave any leaf unturned, she sent his brothers out to kidnap him from the Dominican Friars. As Thomas was resting by the side of a road, his brothers, leading a troop of soldiers, accosted him and brought him to the castle of Monte San Giovanni.

He was kept in solitary confinement with only the visits of his very worldly sister Marotta[9]. His family did everything to force him to change his mind. When their less than gentle persuasion did not work, they went to more and more extreme measures. All seemed to fail.

In the meantime, St. Thomas, not one to waste time, used his time well; he studied. He learned a great deal of the Bible by heart. He wrote a treatise on the *fallacies* of the philosopher Aristotle.

His family was not happy. Things were not going according to plan. Bring in the *Artillery*! His brothers came up with a new and really desperate scheme; they sent a woman of highly questionable character and morals into his

---

[9]Marotta-became converted by her brother St. Thomas Aquinas and she later became a Benedictine Nun and Abbess at Capua, Italy. After her death, she appeared to St. Thomas and asked him to offer Masses for her release from Purgatory.

room. As the poor unsuspecting woman-for-hire made her advances, hoping to seduce Thomas, she was threatened by Thomas, waving wildly a burning brand from the fireplace. Fully understanding his intention was not like hers, he succeeded in chasing her out of the room. After all, if he was not going to cooperate, she might as well flee for her life. She wasn't *absolutely* sure whether he wanted her to go, or to hurt her. She was not going to wait around and ask!

We are told, St. Thomas immediately fell into a deep sleep. As he was peacefully sleeping he had a vision of two *Angels*. The two Heavenly Visitors fastened a *spiritual* chastity belt around his waist which would protect him from all attacks of lust from the fallen angels.

St. Thomas endured two more years of incarceration before his family finally gave up, and he returned to his beloved fellow Dominicans.

St. Margaret of Cortona-(1247-1297 A.D.)

In one of our Lord's appearances to St. Margaret, He said, "*You are the third light granted to the Order of My beloved Francis. He was the first, among the Friars Minor; Clare was the second, among the Nuns; you shall be the third, in the Order of Penance.*"

She was born, in 1247, on a small farm in the Tuscany Region of Italy. Her mother died when she was only seven years old, and she was left with a father who soon remarried. Margaret could count on little love and understanding in her home, as her step-mother was very stern, and her father was completely dominated by this strong woman.

It was no wonder that Margaret would fall for a rather good looking young man from Montepulciano (Italy) and agree to elope with him. It soon became obvious his promises to marry her were empty, at best. But Margaret had become used to the life of luxury he provided for her, in addition to the affection he so lavishly bestowed upon her.

It was not bad enough she lived this life, but she brazenly flaunted herself and her way of life before all the townspeople. She was faithful to her lover and they had one son. She appeared very happy until, one day, her young man failed to return from inspecting one of his estates. Her worrying grew to all-out panic when his dog returned without him. It is said the dog pulled at her dress and brought her to the place where he had been buried. She wept as she looked upon his once beautiful body now grotesquely mutilated.

She took this as a sign of how his and her soul had become in the Eyes of God. She sold all the gifts she had received from her lover, gave them to his family and to the poor, and she and her small son left Montepulciano for her father's farm. She knocked on his door, and dressed in the clothes of a penitent, she begged his forgiveness, pleading she and her son be allowed to live with him. At the cold and unforgiving insistence of the step-mother, he refused.

She was on the edge of despair when she remembered the Friars Minor of Cortona and their well-known reputation for kindness and compassion to sinners. When she and her son arrived in Cortona, she was befriended by two women who took them in and introduced Margaret to the Friars Minor. Margaret did not have an easy time of it, even with the spiritual direction of the two Friars who gently led her back to right relationship with her God. For three *long* years she had strong temptations of the flesh because as the saying goes, *"The spirit is willing but the flesh is weak."*

She journeyed to Laviano, the little town of her birth, and during Mass, asked the entire congregation to forgive her past life.

She would have marched through the streets of Montepulciano with a rope around her neck and her face mutilated, but her spiritual directors felt this too excessive and would not permit it. But in Montepulciano, as in

Laviano, she was allowed to go before the congregation, confess her sins and ask their forgiveness.

It is said, St. Peter wept so long, and so hard, for his denial of Jesus, that all the tears he shed made deep ruts in his face. And so, it was with Margaret. She cared for the sick, the poor, and spent every spare moment in prayer and mortification. She moved out of the comfort of the house of the two ladies who had offered her shelter when she had first come to Montepulciano. She and her son moved into a very modest cottage and subsisted solely on alms. Like St. Francis, before her, she gave all the unbroken bread and the best food to the poor, keeping scraps for herself and her son.

She joined the Third Order of St. Francis, and sent her son went away to school to Arezzo. He remained there until he entered the Franciscan Order. It was as if, not desiring any consolation and wanting to do retribution for her sins, she would not even allow herself the love and companionship of her son.

The Lord not only forgave her, but He repeatedly sent her *Guardian Angel* to tell her so. Like with the rest of us, she could not understand how the Lord could forgive her, how He could shed such light, show such compassion, offer such consolation and bestow so many charisms[10] on her, a sinner.

One day, our Lord and His Angel appeared to her. When He tried to reassure her, Margaret cried out, "*I have been darkness; I have been darker than night!*"

Can you imagine the look of Love on our Savior's Face, as once again, as with Mary Magdalene, He spoke the words of consolation and forgiveness. "*Margaret,*" He said, "*For love of you, new light, I bless the little cell where you live concealed in My Love.*"

---

[10]charisms-gifts of the Holy Spirit

St. Margaret's Guardian Angel not only helped her to discover the path the Lord had chosen for her, that Mystical road that would bring her to closer union with Him, but the sign posts along the way. Her Angel said,

"You are like a house which has been set on fire; it will burn until it is completely consumed; thus you will remain in the fire of tribulation to the very end. Surrounded as you are in peace, you actually live in a state of war. Remember that gold is purified in the furnace."

Was he referring to the suspicions that would travel through the town about her and the Friars, especially the two who were her Spiritual Directors? Those who had been calling her *Saint* wanted to run her out of town; at best, they avoided her as if she were still living her former life of sin. When that didn't work, they whispered and then they made sure it got to the Franciscan Order. Her closest Spiritual Director, Friar Giunta was sent away. Margaret was alone.

Or was she? She continued to have apparitions of her Guardian Angel and the Lord, with messages not only for herself but for others, as well. Her Angel had begun his teaching with the Good Friday part of her walk with the Lord, that of suffering; then, after she accepted it fully, he raised her up to the Easter Sunday part of her Mystical union with her Lord.

The Angel told her that God waits for the heart, from the time of its first desire of Him. When that heart longs for Him passionately, He no longer delays returning to that soul. Love then achieves, in a *moment*, what is accomplished only *in time* in souls of less devotion. The Angel told her, the faithful and fiery soul draws God to herself: when the soul feels empty of all Divine love; when she cannot feel God's Love, then only God can console her. But before He enters this soul so precious to Him, that He so carefully fashioned, he purifies it of *all* illusions. Then and only then, the soul will find her Beloved, her Lord, in everything that happens, everywhere she goes.

Toward the end of her life, her reward for all the good she had done, was rejection and suspicion, emotional pains accompanied by physical; separated from any human companionship, her long torturous days were only surpassed by the loneliness of night; she did not even have sleep as a consolation.

As she was growing closer to going Home to be with her Lord and Companion, He appeared to her. Our Lord said, *"Show how you are converted; call others to repentance....The graces I have bestowed on you are not meant for you alone."* Although discouraged before, *after* her Lord's words she set out with new energy and determination. She was responsible for many of the fallen-away to return to the Sacraments; feuds between family, neighbors and towns were settled; people were called to do penance for their sins.

Friar Giunta returned to give Margaret her last rites. She passed away at fifty years of age. She had spent twenty-nine years doing penance for nine years of sin as a young woman. On the day of her death, the townspeople declared her overwhelmingly a *Saint*. She was formally canonized, raised to the Communion of Saints in 1728.

On May 13th, 1981, as we were traveling through Europe, tracing the lives of the Saints, we discovered Saint Margaret. Her body is under the altar of the church which replaced the one originally built right after her death. *Her body has never decomposed and is incorrupt.* Did our Guardian Angel send us there? What do you think?

St. Catherine of Siena (1347-1380)
Catherine becomes a Third Order Dominican

She privately took the vows of Nuns who belonged to *Religious Orders*, poverty, chastity and obedience, although as a Third Order Dominican, it was not required of her. She

St. Catherine of Siena, Doctor of the Church, Mystic, and Stigmatist, shown here in Ecstasy

stayed in her room, a recluse, except to attend Mass. For three years she lived this solitary life, scourging herself three times a day, denying herself sleep and adequate nourishment, not seeing or hearing anything or anyone outside this little world of hers. Although she allowed no one in her cell, she was never alone. Jesus, sometimes accompanied by His Mother and other times by Saints and *Angels*, would come and instruct her about God His Father, the Truths of the Gospel, about salvation and sin.

But, Jesus and His Heavenly Companions were not her only spirited visitors. The *fallen angels*, with their lies and deceptions, never failed to take an opportunity to attack. Catherine turned to prayer; the demons only howled the louder making it impossible to pray. They appeared in all forms of lewd behavior, attacking her mind with all sorts of sexual thoughts and desires. Not even by closing her eyes, could she block out the filthy work of these demons. She scourged herself all through the night. Still, the barrage of offenses came crashing down on her head and soul. They let her have it again and again, with the *idiocy of this life*, how wonderful and natural it would be to be *a wife and a mother*. One night, drenched and drained from the battle that had been ruthlessly ensuing, *she had a thought* from the Holy Spirit. She remembered the day she had asked the Lord for the *gift of Fortitude.* (*Author's note: I have become more careful what gifts I ask from the Lord, based on whether I am prepared to accept the test.*) The Lord's words came back to her, "*If you want to have the strength to overcome all the enemy's attacks, take the Cross as your refreshment.*" Fortified by the Lord's words, she stood ground, to do battle with the little devils.

Finally giving up, the demons dispersed. The Lord appeared for the *first* time since the attacks had begun. Was Catherine upset! She asked the Lord where He had been during the onslaught. I wonder if He wasn't smiling a little, enjoying the little spitfire He had chosen for a bride, as He replied, "*I was in your heart.*" Catherine, no different than the rest of us, could not understand how the enemy could be attacking her if her Lord was there, and she told Him so. He responded by asking her if her temptations brought her enjoyment or sorrow. She told Him of her feelings of repulsion and her intense trial. He told her, it was He who planted those feelings of displeasure. If *He* had not been in the center of her heart, the thoughts and temptations of the enemy would have pleased her instead of displeasing her. She (or is it we) was to learn a hard lesson, one she was never to forget, God is always with us, even when we do not *feel* Him.[11]

St. Joan of Arc (1412 - 1431)

Joan of Arc is a strong contradiction in our Church and our world. She was abandoned by the country she had fought so hard to protect; she was condemned by a corrupt bishop of the Church to which she pledged undying loyalty. After her death, that same country made her into a heroine; that same Church made her into a Saint. She is now, with St. Thérèse of Lisieux, co-patroness of France. She was the Little Flower's heroine during Thérèse's lifetime. Little did Thérèse realize they would someday share the same title as Patron Saint of France. And although Joan lived some 460 years before St. Thérèse, she was only canonized five years before the Little Flower.

Joan of Arc was illiterate. She could not read nor write. Yet her story is so fascinating that great authors of the Nineteenth and Twentieth centuries, George Bernard Shaw, and Mark Twain, have both written about her. She was not stupid by any means, only unschooled.

---

[11]short excerpt from chapter-St. Catherine of Siena, "*Saints and other Powerful Women in the Church*"

St. Joan of Arc, co-patron Saint of France

There is such an amazing scope to this teenage saint, we cannot get into it in this book, because this is a book on Angels in the lives of the Saints. Our next book will be *Saints and Other Powerful Women in the Church, Part II*, and we will write about Joan of Arc at length, in that book, if the Lord wills it. But for now, let's talk about Joan of Arc and the Angels.

Joan was a peasant girl, daughter of a farmer. Her village of Domremy was sort of a border town. At any given time, it could be part of France, Burgundy, or the Holy Roman Empire, based on who was in charge. Burgundy had sworn allegiance to England, which made things all the worse. Her country was at war with England, the Hundred Year's War, and had been since long before she was born.

While Joan was used to the idea of war, having lived with it all her life, she and her family had to hide out many times when invading soldiers came to their little village *from wherever*, to loot and pillage. These *soldiers* were not really troops for the most part. They were bandits who justified their way of life by posing as soldiers. They roamed in packs, and took advantage of any weakness they could find. (Their modern equivalent would be *terrorists*, cowards who terrorize the unarmed civilian population.) While these Fifteenth century terrorists had no courage, they had weapons, so Joan and her family found themselves running for refuge from the attacks.

Considering the conditions of her country, Joan lived a relatively normal life She was an exceptionally loving, religious, trusting girl. That may have been her great mistake, *trusting people*. But she trusted mostly in the Lord. He was in charge of her life. She spent a lot of time at Church, receiving the Sacraments whenever she could. While she was very holy, she was also the life of the party. She loved to take part in village activities. But her strongest pull was towards God and things of Heaven. She was told many stories of the Saints by her dear mother. Remember, she never learned to read or write. It wasn't really necessary for a girl of her station. She had a special secret place all her own, out in the woods, a little chapel where a statue of our Lady and the Baby Jesus presided. She spent a lot of time in that chapel, praying for her family and her country. Joan was a very patriotic girl. She loved her country and her king, even though she was not sure who he was.

Her years of joy were shortlived. At age twelve, her famous *voices* began coming to her. They were always accompanied by a brilliant flash of light, and came at the precise time the sexton rang the church bells. At first, there was only one voice. When this voice spoke to her, the third time, she knew it was *St. Michael the Archangel*. This was affirmed to her on that third visit by an apparition, she recognized as St. Michael in the company of other Angels. At first, the voice just gave her instructions on how to live a good Christian life. Basically, the Angel told her to be good, go to Church often, and obey her parents. These were good instructions, but to be honest, she was already practicing these virtues.

At a given point, St. Michael advised her she would be visited by St. Margaret of Antioch, and St. Catherine of Alexandria. He told her she had to listen to their instructions, and follow them to the letter. She agreed to do this. When they came, they were beautiful. They wore crowns on their heads. We get the impression that all she could see of them were from their heads down to their waist. Joan grew very comfortable with her Heavenly Visitors, especially St. Michael, to whom she and much of the world of the Middle Ages had a great devotion.

But a time was to come when the messages took on a different tone. She was shocked when she was told, *"Daughter of God, you must leave your village and go to*

France."[12] She replied "*But I'm only a young girl, and I cannot ride or fight.*" She was told she was to save France from the English. This was all beyond her. Think about it, though. This girl was a teenager. Granted, she was much more spiritual than most adults of her time. But she was being told things that most adults would have a major problem accepting. Given the same set of circumstances, I don't know anyone who wouldn't be completely bowled over by the proposition set before this young girl.

She knew they were sincere. She *trusted*, especially in St. Michael. She knew he would not allow the evil one to deceive her. But she was very confused. As the years progressed, the messages became more specific. She would save France from defeat at the hands of the British. This continued until she was sixteen years old. Her voices would give her no peace. Then, one day in May, she was given a direct command. She was told by St. Michael to go to a Robert de Baudricourt, in a neighboring town, and tell him to provide her with troops, to escort her to the Dauphin[13]. His first reaction upon seeing this young peasant girl, wearing her worn red dress, and claiming she would save France and have the Dauphin crowned king, was to give her a swift boot. Instead, he ordered her uncle (who had brought her), to take her home. She returned to Domremy, completely crushed.

Her Angelic voices would not leave her alone! She pleaded and tried to explain how she had only been able to accomplish *humiliation* at the hands of Robert De Baudricourt; but St. Michael would have none of it. Finally, he said to her, "*It is God who commands it!*" Fortified by the courage and determination of the Angel, she set out, at the

---

[12]At that time, Domremy may have been part of Lorraine, the Holy Roman Empire, or Burgundy.

[13]The only legitimate heir to the French throne, but he was in hiding for fear of being executed by the British.

beginning of the following year, to see Robert de Baudricourt, once again. However, by this time the situation of the French was so disastrous, he was not anxious to dismiss her. He was ready to grab onto any hope. Finally, he gave in, and assigned three men to bring her to the king.

Everything she did for the next fifteen months was orchestrated by the voice of St. Michael. She could do no wrong. She was given a white suit of armor. The banner she carried into combat was that of *Jesus and Mary*. Every battle she fought, the French won by a wide margin. The English were pushed back.

The English offered a ransom for the capture of Joan of Arc, dead or alive. But no one could get close to her. She was able to overcome the politics of the French court, to have the Dauphin crowned King of France.

But then it was over for Joan. Her mission was completed, as far as the instructions of the Angel were concerned. What then, prompted her to continue going into battle, when she had not been instructed to do so? Whatever the reason, all her future battles were disasters for the French and for Joan. She was even allowed to be captured by her enemies, the Burgundians. They put her up for ransom. Her French king, the Dauphin she had placed on the throne, abandoned her. She was not worth putting up a franc. But, the English, who hated her, put up a sum equivalent to about $50,000, so that they could humiliate and *execute* her. They were able to get a corrupt French bishop, who had ambitions, to set up a mock trial, at which Joan was condemned as a heretic, and ultimately burned at the stake.

We have an important question to reflect on here. Why did Joan continue doing battle? As far as her voices were concerned, she should not have. Had she lost her focus? Was she now battling for God, or for herself? Was there a certain amount of self-gratification from winning all those battles? She had become the heroine of France at nineteen years old. She was a very dramatic figure. Was her head turned even a little by the adulation she was receiving? Was she looking for man's approval? Better yet, was she looking for approval from the misfit she had made king?

If *any* of the above were true, the results would have been predictable. She began working on her own agenda, not the Lord's as transmitted to her by the Angel Michael. Is that why everything she did became a catastrophe? Is that why her king abandoned her, without even attempting to rescue her from their enemies? Did St. Michael abandon her? During her last great trial, when it became obvious, she was to be the victim of a kangaroo court, did Michael come to her rescue once more, at the end? We're told that at one point, she backed off from her claims that she had truly heard Angelic voices give her instructions. She was given a period of respite. But soon after, she resumed her claim with strength and fervor, knowing she would be burned at the stake, as a *witch*.

In the account of her death, it is reported that she was allowed to have a crucifix held up so she could look at it, as the raging flames hungrily darted up the pole, mercilessly anxious and ready to devour her body. She seemed to go into an ecstasy, oblivious of the red hot flames that were closing in on her, enveloping her, attacking the young body of the former standard bearer and soldier of Jesus and Mary, and France. Everyone waited anxiously to see her react to the fire, to hear her cry out for mercy. *But she didn't. It was as if she didn't feel any pain!* Then, something unusual happened at her execution. One of the spectators, the secretary to King Henry, cried out, as Joan was dying, "*We are lost; we have burned a saint!*"

Is it possible, that although she had disobeyed him, at the end, her Angel, her Michael, came to her rescue? Could he have stretched out his massive wings and covered the body of this little girl who had trusted him so completely?

Did he protect her from the flames, so that she experienced no pain, as her body was destroyed, and her soul was lifted up to Heaven?

We believe St. Michael the Archangel, and very possibly a legion of Angels were there, to bring their sister Home, after her hard battle. We know the Lord was protecting her. But we have to trust that He was more interested in her soul than her body.

We don't understand the Lord's ways. We don't know why He allowed Joan of Arc to suffer the way she did. But we know that He loves us, that He wants nothing more than to lift all of us up into Glory. Do we hear Angelic voices the way Joan did? Do we listen to their instructions? Do we respond the way she did? Do we trust our souls to their bidding? The time may be coming, indeed it may be here, when the salvation of our souls will depend on how strictly we obey their directives. *Think about it!*

St. Frances of Rome-wife, mother and Saint (1384-1440)

The Great Western Schism began and the Church needed a Saint, someone willing to live and die, if necessary, for the Church. In 1384, Jesus was to raise up such a Saint. A little girl, Frances, was born in Rome, of the nobility. This Schism was to cause Frances and her family much pain. She never lived to see unity within the Church.

When Frances was only eleven years old, her desire was to become a Nun. Her parents, meaning well, arranged a suitable marriage with someone of her class. She gave in to her parents and was married at thirteen.

She had many children. Although she was very fervent in her prayer life, when her husband or her children called out to her, she put it all aside and tended to their needs, always faithful to her vocation as a wife and mother. Like St. Teresa of Avila, who found God "*among the pots and pans*", she could and did find God in her household duties, whether doing housework, cooking or wiping her children's runny noses. She never judged how she was best serving the Lord. She just said an ongoing "*yes*"!

In 1411, Saint Frances' son Evangelista became critically ill from the plague that had swept the region. He was barely nine years old. Before he died, he smiled up to his mother and said, "*Behold the Angels who have come to take me to Heaven! Mother, I will remember you!*"

One year after Evangelista died, as St. Frances was praying in the Oratory of her palace in Rome, a brilliant light cut through the dawn, flooding the room. As she adjusted her eyes, she could see her son Evangelista in the light. He was wearing the same clothes he had been wearing when they had laid him to rest. His features were unchanged except to be *more* radiant and breathtakingly beautiful.

He was accompanied by what appeared to be another boy. Although this boy outshone her son in looks and stature, she had eyes only for her boy. Evangelista held out his outstretched arms to his mother. He told his mother he had come to console her, that he was in Heaven and happy. Like St. Paul and many of the saints, Evangelista said Heaven was beyond any description he could make.

"*My companion is an Archangel,*" he said, "*and I occupy a place with him among the Angels of the Second Choir of the first Hierarchy.*" Evangelista was careful to add, his Angel occupied a place higher than his; but that God, in His generosity, had sent His Angel to *her*, to be her comfort in her long hard, sad journey on earth. He told her she would be able to see the Angel with her own eyes. As she tried to hold on to him, Evangelista said, he had to leave, but whenever she looked at the Angel, she would be reminded of him and she would be comforted.

Before departing, he paused for a moment; he looked at her. His eyes became sad. He said he had another reason for coming to her. He told her, his sister Agnes would soon be joining him in Heaven. But, he reassured her, this Angel, whom the Lord had sent to Frances, would be her companion for the next twenty-three years.

The vision lasted an hour. Her son left, and true to his word, there was the Angel, arms crossed over his chest, standing in front of her. She fell down on her knees and thanked God for this precious gift. She then begged the Angel to protect her from the onslaughts of the fallen angels who filled her with doubts of all kinds, to help her handle the difficult moments in her life, and to guide her in perfecting herself so that one day, she would be with her God and her son in Paradise.

Soon after, Agnes' health began to deteriorate, and a year later, at sixteen years old, she was dead. The grieving mother's only consolation was the Angel beside her. No one but she could see him. And when she committed a sin, *she* no longer could, until she was repentant and confessed her transgressions.

Frances could not look directly at him; he was so brilliant he was blinding. She had to keep her eyes fastened on the aura encompassing his body. Those times when she was either deep in prayer, or under attack by the devil, or when she mentioned the Angel to her confessor, the Angel would allow Frances to look straight at him. She said he resembled a boy of about nine years old. His eyes twinkled and danced as he looked at her. He had the kindest, most loving expression on his face. His hair was like fine golden yarn. It reached down his neck and shoulders. The light from his hair enabled Frances to read her Office at night.

The Angel seemed to have his power in his hair. Whenever the devil tried to attack Frances, the Angel shook his hair effortlessly and a little disdainfully and the devil trembled and fled. Through the Angel, she could see into men's hearts, and discern when the devil was in charge of the soul before her, or God. The Angel walked always before her, to the right of her and to the left of her, over her and beneath her, always there to protect her.

Frances' husband's love and admiration grew greater, as he grew older. One day, knowing how very much she had wanted to be a Nun, he told her he would release her from her wifely duties, if she would remain under his roof. Frances fulfilled her dream; she formed a community of women living in the world, without religious vows, who would consecrate themselves to God and to the care of the poor and the sick. It was not until her husband died and was laid to rest between their two children, Evangelista and Agnes, did Frances join her community.

On the day she joined the community that she had founded, the *Oblates of Mary*, she had a vision of our Lord. He was seated on a high throne, surrounded by myriads of Angels worshiping Him. When the Angelic Choir of the Powers came before the Lord, He pointed to one of the highest of their Order and assigned him to take the place of the Archangel who had been St. Frances' companion these last twenty-three years. This Angel was more beautiful than the other and possessed even more power to fight the devil. By his presence alone, he was able to chase the fallen angels from St. Frances. This Angel who remained with St. Frances for the next four years, brought her three golden palms; they represented the three virtues he would stress over and over again in Frances: that of charity, firmness and prudence.

It was March the 9th, 1440. Everyone had been around her bed for seven days. It was obvious, she was dying. Night had settled on the room. Before they could light a candle, *suddenly* a bright light lit up her face. *"The Angel has finished his task. He beckons me to follow him."* And with this, she died. All the faithful whose lives she had so powerfully touched, and those seeking miraculous cures, filed into the palace. They became so numerous, she had to be moved to the church of Santa Maria Nuova. As news of miracles spread throughout Rome and then Italy, the church could barely contain all who came in thanksgiving and in petition. She was laid to rest in the chapel of the church reserved for her community.

Her community, the Oblates of Mary are still in existence and still wear the clothes of the noble ladies of Saint Frances' time.

In 1608, Frances was recognized by the Church and raised officially to the Communion of Saints. The church where she is buried was renamed Santa Francesca Romana.

Neither one of the two Angels who were her companions for the last twenty-seven years of her life was her Guardian Angel. As St. Thomas Aquinas said, when someone is chosen to lead or to direct others in the way of holiness, he or she is given *additional* Angels of a higher Choir. And so, it was with Saint Frances. Imagine the Angels, Pope John Paul II has to help him, in the tremendous task he has.

St. Teresa of Avila-heart pierced by an Angel (1515-1582)

St. Teresa struggled to find a Priest who could understand her apparitions of the Lord. At last, she found such a Priest.

Her consolation in this Priest was short-lived, as were most earthly gifts in Teresa's life. He was transferred, because the Nuns were suspicious of Teresa having a non-Carmelite hearing her confession.

Teresa had the love and joy of having her sister Juana staying at the Incarnation. Even that, one of the last of her beloved ties with her family, was to be severed as her sister Juana left the Incarnation to be married.

Through her Spiritual Director, Teresa learned she would have to give up even the smallest attachments, if she wished to please her Lord Jesus. As she followed her director's advice to pray to the Holy Spirit, *Veni Creator*, she

*St. Teresa of Avila received a Transverberation of the Heart.
She saw an Angel to the left of her. He was small and very
beautiful. He had a long golden dart in his hand, with what
appeared to be fire at the end of it. He thrust it into her Heart
several times, piercing her down to her innermost organs,
leaving her burning with a great love for God.*

went into a rapture where the Lord said to her, "*I desire you no longer converse with men, but with Angels.*" From then on, although she was warm and caring, joyful and present to her Sisters, she belonged only to her Lord Jesus.

Two years later, she received, what she called, a terrifying caress, a *Transverberation of her heart*[14]. She saw an Angel to the left of her. He was small and very beautiful. He was so illuminated, he had to be one of the very highest of the Angels, the Cherubim. He had a long golden dart in his hand, with what appeared to be fire at the end of it. She said he thrust it into her heart several times, piercing her down to her innermost organs, leaving her burning with a great love for God.

After St. Teresa's death, when they investigated her heart, it appeared to be pierced through the center as if by a dart. In 1872, at the request of the Prioress at Alba de Tormes, three physicians, professors of medicine and surgery at the University of Salamanca, examined Teresa's heart. They found the heart still incorrupt and untouched by the ravages of death, after almost *three hundred years*. The heart was punctured on both sides, leaving a perforation above the left and right auricles, verifying what Teresa had said. *(Author's note: When we visit Alba de Tormes, the Convent where she died and where she asked to be buried, we can still see and venerate the miraculously preserved heart of St. Teresa, with the stab wound of the Angel's dart.)*

After the Transverberation, Teresa's raptures became more and more frequent. She would see Christ in the Eucharist during Mass, especially after receiving Communion. She would go into ecstasy, no longer being

---

[14]Transverberation-(a)Teresa's mystical experience of the piercing of her heart which occurred in 1559. (b)On May 25, 1726, Pope Benedict XIII appointed a festival and office for the Transverberation, which is observed on August 27th. It was first instituted by the Carmelites and then later celebrated throughout all Spain.

able to feel her body, with a weightlessness that lifted her whole body into the air, called *Levitation*. Some of her Nuns testified that one day they saw her body rise high above the window from which she had received the Host from the Bishop of Avila. Teresa was thoroughly embarrassed when this occurred in front of others, not wanting to be judged *holy*. In response to her requests for anonymity, our Lord would gift her with such outward signs of radiant beauty, it was impossible not to see her gifts of sanctity. Jesus loves to be playful with His children. He enjoys them so, like Teresa, in their human simpleness, finding them forever *"precious."*

†

As Teresa was preparing to open her first house, the Convent of Saint Joseph, even the most supportive of her friends began to have doubts, not only did the Lord come to fortify her, but St. Clare of Assisi, as well, along with the Blessed Mother on her right and St. Joseph on her left. They pledged to help, reassuring her of their intercession with the Lord. They made no secret of how delighted they were with her, their love radiating, warming her. *As she saw the Angels carrying them Heavenward,* she knew her Jesus had called out the heavenly artillery just in time. *Our eleventh hour God came to the rescue once again!*

†

Saint Teresa and her Nuns always travelled at night to found new houses. In that way, there would not be too much fanfare as they entered a town. The enemies of Christ have always been diligent in their attempts to stop those who would bring the Gospel life to the world. As it was not safe for young women, or for that matter *women*, to travel at night, alone, you might ask how did Saint Teresa *dare* choose to do so. The *Angels*, she said, lighted the way, leading them, guiding and protecting them over every hill, through every dark street into the next unknown place to which the Lord was calling them.

With the Angels always there, not only as they journeyed, but remaining with them, Saint Teresa and her Reformed Discalsed Carmelite Nuns were to bring much needed *reform* to their Order and to the Church. Born the very year, 1515, another member of our Church, Martin Luther brought about division and dissension through disobedience (probably listening to the fallen angels), Saint Teresa, guided by her Guardian Angel and probably other Higher Angels assigned to her, said "*yes*" over and over again. And no matter what Satan, through often *good men* misguided, did to her, her faithfulness to Mother Church, and her Angel, made her a Saint and a Doctor of the Church.[15]

St. John Bosco (Don Bosco) (1815-1888)

When St. John Bosco dedicated the famous Marian Shrine, in Turin, Italy, Our Lady Help of Christians, he used three different types of choral groups. This was to enrich the music with a fullness, a strength and an intensity that would resound throughout the church, filling it and the people, the Mystical Body of the Church.

Standing on one side of the Sanctuary was a choir of all males. They represented the *Church Militant*. They sang of hope in the midst of the hopelessness, the sorrow and suffering on earth.

On the other side of the Sanctuary was a second male choir. They represented the *Poor Souls* in Purgatory as they intoned their desire and yearning to be with the Lord and His Heavenly Kingdom.

But right in the middle, directly under the high dome, were two hundred of the sweetest, most angelic voices. There was not a male voice amongst them. St. John Bosco used all female voices to represent the *Angels of Paradise*.

---

[15]On October the 4th, 1970, Pope Paul the VI proclaimed Teresa and Catherine of Siena Doctors of the Church.

And *they* had not coerced him into doing so. He freely chose the young women for this mission...or did he?

Don Bosco and il Grigio (the gray one)

Making the statement, "*The chapter would not be complete without....*" becomes a pat phrase, when speaking of Don Bosco. Il Grigio, the gray dog, really had nothing to do with Don Bosco's ministry, but very possibly, he had a lot to do with his ability to *perform* his ministry. Don Bosco actually devoted the last chapter of his autobiography, *Memoirs of the Oratory*, to his good friend, Il Grigio. So if it was important enough for the master to talk about him, we can also share about the gray dog.

We have to preface it by telling you that a lot of people didn't like Don Bosco, probably more *hated* him than *loved* him. Attempts on Don Bosco's life became a commonplace occurrence. Either dissident *religious* groups wanted to get him, or *political* groups. But between the two, he really had to be on his toes. It got to the point where he could pretty well sense when he was being set up for an attempt on his life. Usually, someone would come and ask him to go to the home of a sick person, to administer the last sacraments of the Church. That's where he was most vulnerable. Most times, he would try to bring two or more of his four strong young people with him for protection. But there were times, when he was alone on the street, or was not able to bring anyone with him. That's when he would find *Il Grigio*. No one ever knew where he came from, or where he would go after the incidents.

The first instance took place in 1854, when Don Bosco was returning home late at night. He was in a very bad section of Turin. He saw two men in front of him, walking slowly, keeping up with his pace. He wasn't sure they were after him, but as he speeded up, they speeded up; if he slowed down, they did the same. He crossed to the other side of the street. When they did the same, he knew he was in trouble. He turned around to retreat, but they jumped him and threw a black cloak over his head. He tried to fight them, but it was no use. They were attempting to jam a cloth inside his mouth, when all of a sudden, out of nowhere, a huge, gray, hideous looking *mastiff*[16] emerged from the darkness, and came charging at them. His growls sounded like those of a wolf or a bear. He *lunged* at Don Bosco's attackers. They were frightened right down to their toes. They pleaded with Don Bosco to call him off. He would agree to, when they agreed to stop accosting passersby. They ran for their life. Il Grigio didn't chase them. He stayed by Don Bosco's side.

From that time on, whenever Don Bosco came home late, after he passed the last of the buildings, Il Grigio would come from out of nowhere, to walk him home. Many people from the Oratory saw Il Grigio. One time he barged into the Oratory. Everyone was frightened. But then he ran up to Don Bosco, nuzzled his face into his friend and ran off. Don Bosco never made a big deal about Il Grigio, who he was, where he came from, why he stayed around for *thirty years*.

Don Bosco writes that the last time he saw Il Grigio was in 1866. But he finished writing his memoirs some years before he died, so he did not chronicle all his adventures with Il Grigio. There is a recorded incident that Il Grigio accompanied Don Bosco on the road to Ventimiglia, near the French border, as late as 1883. When Don Bosco shared this with a friend, she marveled, because dogs just don't live that long. Don Bosco smiled and said, *"Well, maybe it was his son or grandson."* He didn't want to get into it with her. The Salesians sisters testified that they experienced Il Grigio's protection, on three occasions *between 1893 and 1930*.

---

[16]Mastiff - a mixed breed - a large, powerful, smooth-coated dog with hanging lips and drooping ears - very often used for watchdogs.

Who or what was Il Grigio? Many Salesians said, *they* had seen him. Did he protect Don Bosco and the Salesians for 80 years? His origins have never been officially investigated, but there are theories. In 1870, Don Bosco commented, "*It sounds ridiculous to call him an Angel, yet he is no ordinary dog...*" Our only comment is, *why not an Angel?*

Saint Gemma Galgani (1878-1903)

People ask about modern day Saints. I do not believe you can find one more so than St. Gemma Galgani. She was born at the end of the 19th century and died at the very beginning of the 20th. When she was born, many people were immigrating to the New World, with hopes in their hearts for a new and better life for their families. In the century in which she died, the world would become so self-centered and sinful, it would develop means of destruction that would kill 26 million babies in a matter of sixteen years (by abortion), rulers would turn deadly gases and bombs on innocent people, including their own countrymen, and dare to call it a "*holy war.*" We tell you this, as this is a story about the battles of St. Gemma's Guardian Angel and the fallen angels. I believe, without our Guardian Angels, we would not be writing this and you would not be reading it.

The various gifts Gemma possessed and the very apparent involvement of her Guardian Angel in her life, were *tested* and retested by her very reliable and holy Spiritual Director, Fr. Germano di S. Stanislao.

Bob and I, along with our family, first heard of St. Gemma when we visited Lucca, Italy, in the late 1970's. We saw first hand many of St. Gemma's writings that had been smeared by the devil. There is on display in her convent, till today, a page where you can see a black hoof print on one of her letters; again, visibly present to attest to what she wrote in her autobiography.

Left:
*St. Gemma Galgani,
Mystic, Stigmatist, in
Ecstasy*

Below:
*St. Gemma, her Angel,
Our Lady and Our
Lord Jesus as she
receives the Stigmata*

St. Gemma had a *personal* relationship with her Guardian Angel. She could see him with her own two eyes, those of her body.[17] They were friends. They talked to each other. They prayed together. He watched over her, as she napped. She wrote, Jesus, true to His Promise that He would never leave us alone, gave her a Guardian Angel who never left her side.

She made an entry in her diary, "*This evening after my confession to Father Vallini, I felt agitated and disturbed: it was a sign the devil was near...*" She went on to say he was very small. But what he lacked in stature and girth, he more than compensated for in his revoltingly hideous appearance. St. Gemma felt herself becoming paralyzed by fear. She continued to pray, only more so. Then she felt punches pummeling her back and shoulders. Although, at times, she thought she would faint from the pain, she never stopped praying. The *enemy* did not let up for a good half hour. It seemed her Guardian Angel was not with her, she thought, or as St. Catherine of Siena said to Jesus, how could this have happened.

When her Angel finally appeared, he asked her why she was so upset. She begged him to stay awake as she slept; she pleaded that she was terribly frightened. He argued playfully, he had to sleep, too. She countered, "*Angels do not sleep.*" He insisted, a twinkle in his eye, that he had to rest, Angel or no, and he wanted to know where. As she slept, he spread his wings above her head and remained there all night. When she awakened the next morning, always true to his word, there he was. St. Gemma wrote of these experiences in her diary, at the direction of her Spiritual Director. She was twenty-two years old and had already received the Stigmata[18].

---

[17]many Saints saw Jesus and the Angels with the eyes of their heart, as a blind man sees.

[18]the Five Bleeding Wounds of Christ

As with so many of us, to whom the Lord gives gifts of one kind or other[19], St. Gemma thought everyone could see their Guardian Angel. She was quite shocked, when she discovered this was not so. At times, it is necessary to *know* that God treats each one of us *individually* or else we do not appreciate the magnitude of every gift He bestows upon us.

She made an entry in her diary on July 23, 1900. She wrote of a bout she had had with the devil. She spoke of the disgusting temptations she'd suffered. She said she found all temptations repulsive, but those against *holy purity* made her feel even more miserable. Having taunted her, the devil left her, and her Guardian Angel returned. He consoled her; he told her, she had done nothing wrong. The sin is not in the temptation, but in the saying *yes* to it.

Relieved, she turned to *him*! Where had he been? He was supposed to stay with her at all times, protecting her. Fine Guardian Angel, he was! It was at times like this, she complained, when she most needed him. Smiling at her, as if she was but a little child, he said that he was with her during the entire battle; he is always with her hovering over her, protecting her. He promised her that our Lord Jesus would visit her that evening.

The Angel dictated to Saint Gemma some very simple guidelines on how to conduct her life, what he expected of her. One of the things that I found notably interesting was, he said, to never offer your opinion unless you are first *asked* for it. He instructed her, it was wisdom to admit you are wrong before someone else brings it to your attention. Another admonition was to be cautious *what* she looked at. With what we watch on television and see in the magazines, the Angel's words pierce us like an arrow. The eyes are the mirror of the soul, but they are also the lens of the soul.

---

[19]an experience of the Holy Spirit whether at Marriage Encounter or at a Curcillo weekend, or at a Charismatic Renewal.

What they see is recorded in our memory. We do not often know why we are depressed, at times. Suddenly, a married man or woman says to his or her spouse, "I no longer want the responsibility of family life. I have to live for *me*! I deserve more." I,I,I, the ego, the looking at self to the exclusion of others.

One day, our young priest told a second grade class preparing to receive their first Sacrament of Penance, that the cause of all sin is selfishness. And yet, that's all our eyes see and learn on television[20]. He also said that these eyes that we expose to all subtle, and sometimes not so subtle, forms of sin are the same eyes that one day will gaze upon Heaven and our Lord and His Mother. It makes you want to cry. Can I look into Your Eyes, Jesus? Will You see what I have seen? We know He will and does now. Will that stop us? As you walk closer to the Lord, on the way to His Kingdom, you will find your spirit becoming more and more troubled by what you see and hear, to the point of so much pain, you will no longer be able to watch what you have been viewing in the past. Do you perhaps have a Guardian Angel who wants to warn you? Or is he warning you, right now?

Saint Gemma's Angel did not go easy with her. Nothing passed by him; no transgression was too small or too trivial. He knew her every thought; whenever her mind wandered as she prayed, he punished her promptly and thoroughly. He did not hesitate to reprimand her, when he judged it was necessary. Was it that the Angel knew he did not have that much time, as this little Saint would not live to an old age?

One day, the Angel looked at her so severely, she began to cry. "*How could you commit such faults in my presence,*" he scolded, his eyes boring a hot coal into her soul. When she looked up at him later, during mealtime, he still glared at

---

[20]except on holy, solid programming like Mother Angelica and EWTN

her. When she tried to avert his eyes, he commanded her to look at him. It got so unbearable, she pleaded to Jesus and His Mother to take her away; she could not stand the Angel's rejection any longer. In the daytime, he'd come up to her over and over again, and say, "*I'm ashamed of you.*" His manner was so severe, she was afraid to say *anything* to him, to even question *what* she had done so wrong. At night, still feeling his disapproval, try as she might, she could not fall asleep. Finally, at three in the morning, her Angel came up to her and said, "*Go to sleep, naughty girl.*"

You might say, and rightly so, if a Saint of the magnitude of Saint Gemma could be considered naughty by an Angel, what are we? Remember, to whom more is given, more is expected. We, as Catholics, have the Grace and the strength of our Sacraments.

The Angel was not always cross with Saint Gemma. On the contrary, her Spiritual Director said he always knew when Saint Gemma was looking at her Angel. She had a look of radiant happiness. She glowed, her eyes fixed on something or someone beyond, as if she was in ecstasy. She seemed to be far off in another place, in another time. But, when she turned her eyes away from the Angel, back to him, her Director, she was her old self again.

Padre Pio was known to tell his spiritual children to send their Guardian Angels to him. In the case of Saint Gemma, she not only sent her Angel to her Spiritual Director with a *message*, but her Angel would return with a *reply*. He travelled as far as from Lucca to Rome (approximately 226 miles), and at times even farther.

It seems, with all the true Mystics, we have studied, they always were ready to have their visions tested; they prayed the apparitions were of God and not a manifestation of the devil, or of their own minds. Any doubts, whether their own or someone else's, they always turned to their Spiritual Directors for advice. When someone implied that possibly this gift, that of her Angel delivering messages to, and bringing back responses from her Director, might be the work of the devil, Saint Gemma immediately brought the matter up to her Director, for his discernment. He told her exactly what to do to block *any* interference from the devil.

Testing her Angel, he directed Saint Gemma to order her Angel *not* to deliver any more messages! But, the Angel *continued* to do so. This disturbed the Director. He enjoined Saint Gemma to pray to Jesus and her Angel that some signs be sent, so he might believe this was the work of the Lord and not the *enemy*. Needless to say, he received the signs, and the Angel continued to deliver Saint Gemma's messages like clock work.

The day Saint Gemma received the Five Bleeding Wounds of our Lord Jesus, her Angel was not only by her side, he gently and lovingly cared for her needs. She wrote in her diary, "*There was pain in my hands and feet and side, and when I got up I saw they were dripping blood. I covered them up as best as I could and, with the help of my Angel, climbed into bed.*"

He was always there for her. She spoke often of their times together, as you would speak of a best friend or a brother. In one of her letters, she spoke of the Angel coming to her just before she began to suffer, one night. She said, she and her Angel had been adoring the Lord in all his Glory and Magnificence. Suddenly, she felt such remorse for her sins, she wanted to run away from her Angel; she was so ashamed. She agonized for what seemed like an eternity. Then, her Angel lifted her up, comforting her, arming her anew with strength for the battles ahead. He held two crowns out to her; one of lilies and one of thorns. He asked Saint Gemma which crown she chose. She replied, she desired "*that of Jesus.*" He handed her the crown of thorns. She wept tears of happiness; she had been chosen to share the Lord's Crown. She kissed the crown over and over, again. Oh Lord, what are our crowns of thorns, and would we cry tears of joy upon receiving them? Would we choose them? Or would we turn on You?

Saint Gemma was not only in the company of her Angel, but others would come to be with her as well; the Angels would bless her in the Name of the Lord; they would pray together. One morning, when she awakened, her Director's Angel was still not there. Having had the Angel with her and her Angel, the night before, when she had fallen asleep, she started to weep uncontrollably. She asked her Director if he would please tell his Angel, if she had done anything to offend him, she was sorry and would never do it again. Would he please send him back? She said, she loved him even though he was more strict with her, than her own Angel.

Have you ever been in a situation where you did not want to go somewhere or see some show, but felt helpless to get out of it? Well, the Saints before you also had these struggles. One night, Saint Gemma's aunts and sister asked her to join them. They said, the distraction would be good for her. She wanted to stay home and pray. She was torn between her family and her Angel. She knew the wishes of her Angel, but she felt obligated to obey her family. She later wrote to her Director, she judged her Angel was not happy with her decision, as he did not accompany her.

She had such a close relationship with the Angel, at times, she was overheard by her Director arguing with him, insisting upon having her way. She took such liberties, her Director cautioned her to use *respect* when she spoke to her Angel. After all, he held a position above all humans (except Mary). From that time on, she was more careful.

Her Angel was with her when she was preparing to go to Confession, reminding her of faults she had not confessed. One time, he gave her those same severe looks we spoke of before. This time, it was that she had hidden some of her

visions and experiences from her confessor. She had not
wanted to talk about herself, judging this might be construed
an act of pride. The Angel's looks sent her back to make a
new and more complete confession. When she met the
Angel, as she stepped out of the confessional, he was smiling.
The night before she had not been feeling well. His smile
now brought new life to the death she felt overtaking her,
during the night.

The devil appeared to her, dressed as a Guardian
Angel. She later told her Angel, although the devil was
dressed like an Angel, she had not obeyed him. Had she
some knowledge of *who* he really was? She did not hesitate
to remonstrate the Angel, at this time, "*Do not loan him your
clothes anymore; let him dress as the devil he is.*" In the lives
of the Saints and those trying to become Saints, the devil
very often comes disguised. He does not even have the
courage to appear as he is; he has to cheat and lie.

Saint Gemma lived her twenty-five years on this earth
with the gift of seeing, hearing and feeling her Angel beside
her. Her story is one of pain and ecstasy, not unlike that of
the other Saints. She suffered *emotionally* from those who
made fun of her, disbelieving her ecstasies, judging her mad,
at best, and a fraud, at worst. She had never-ending physical
suffering, as a result of very poor health. Once on the point
of death, she was cured by an apparition of St. Gabriel of the
Sorrows. She was disappointed in life. She had wanted to
be a Passionist Nun, but although she had been cured, her
medical record prevented her from being admitted into the
Order.

At the end, after a long and very painful illness, our
Lord and His Mother called Saint Gemma *Home.* Saturday,
April the 11th, 1903, Saint Gemma *peacefully* breathed her
last sigh. Because of the accounts of her life, written by her
Spiritual Directors, people began to pray for her
intercession, shortly after Saint Gemma's death.

Rather than enhance her cause, it met much opposition *because* of the phenomena and extraordinary occurrences in her life. Although it seemed it would delay all attempts to proclaim her a Saint, the Congregation of Rites did declare that Saint Gemma was worthy to be declared part of the Communion of Saints because of the the *Christian virtues* she practiced in a most heroic fashion. They have never passed judgment on any of the phenomena, or, as we like to say, the miraculous occurrences in her life.

In 1933, she became Blessed Gemma. In 1940, the Church had a new Saint. Saint Gemma has a tremendous following and not only in her native Italy, but in the rest of the world.

†

There are many saints and beatas who have had experiences with the Angels, as well as religious and laity. We could dedicate an entire book to the intercession of the Angels in the lives of humans here on earth. Perhaps we will, one day, if the Lord gives us time. We pray that you'll read about these saints' lives in their entirety. We have only been able to give you thumbnail sketches of their lives, with particular emphasis on their encounters with the Heavenly Hosts. Most of the saints we've either written about, or will be writing about them in our forthcoming books. Remember, they are your heritage, your relatives. Take advantage of the gift of their lives. They were lived for you.

Left:
*Pope John XXIII
reigned 1958-1963*

Above:
*Pope Paul VI
reigned 1963-1978*

Left:
*Pope John Paul I
reigned 33 days
1978*

The Popes and the Angels

St. Catherine of Siena called the Popes, "*Sweet Christ on Earth.*" As Catholics, do we not believe that the Holy Spirit has chosen our Popes for His Church and that having done so, inspires them with interpretation of the Truth as handed down to us from our Lord Jesus Christ Himself?

The battle lines are drawn! The battle lines have always been drawn! We have on one side those who are *above* the teachings of the Church passed on to us for close to two thousand years. And then on the other side, we have those of us who believe in the Word, the teachings of the Magisterium and the traditions of our Church. For this, we are often called simple and naive, behind the times, orthodox. And I admit, until you study a little more, they can have you going. Stabs at your heart, like "*No one believes in the Angels, anymore*", especially when uttered by someone you respect, I admit, can lead you to wondering what is true.

I cannot explain the utter and complete joy in my heart when I began to research the stand the *Popes* have taken on the Angels down through the centuries.

Pope Pius XI

Pope Pius XI confided he prayed to his Guardian Angel every day, morning, noon and night. And when things got rough, as they often do in the life of the Fisherman, he prayed in between those times.

He had great need of his Guardian Angel and had no problem confiding his need and dependency on his Angel. Lest it be a secret, the Pope declared at a public audience that he turned to his Guardian Angel, to give him the strength to stand up to the tyranny of his day.

Not one to compromise, Pope Pius XI came out against Stalin and his heartless brutalization of anyone who thought differently than he, or someone who simply had land and power he wanted. He challenged the anti-Christ of his day, Adolf Hitler, warning the world of this madman's insatiable anger and lust for power. He bravely stood up to Mussolini. As leaders of conquered nations *corroborated* with their invaders for expediency's sake, this brave Pope stood, as if at the front of a huge army and defied not only Mussolini, the dictator in his own backyard, but his henchman buddy Hitler.

He did not keep the intercession of his Guardian Angel as a private devotion of his, alone, but would counsel others to do, likewise. He especially recommended it to those doing battle on the front lines, to the diplomatic corp of the Holy See and of nations, to teachers responsible for the formation of ideas in the young, to missionaries bringing the Word and the Love of Jesus Christ very often to people who never heard or saw a Christian before.

Pope Pius XI spoke to Monsignor *Angelo* Roncalli, (who was years later to become Pope John XXIII) about the Angels, on one of his visits to the Holy See. He explained that the Angels take delight in protecting us, making smooth our paths, solving our problems, and knocking out all opposition.

As Monsignor *Angelo* Roncalli, John the XXIII served in countries for many years where there were few Catholics. Ecumenism was not popular round the world and the Church was persecuted. He had an up-hill fight all the way.

Pope Pius XI told Monsignor Roncalli that whenever he was going into dialogue with someone whose mind was closed, who would not listen or bend even the slightest, he, the Pope sent his Guardian Angel to speak to his opponent's Guardian Angel, to discuss the problem with him. After the two Angels had come to an understanding, the Pope said, the meeting between him and his adversary went much smoother.

Pope Pius XI, two days before his death, spoke on the Angels. His encyclical on the Angels stands as evidence of the Pope's strong emphasis of dependency on the Angels. I must admit I knew little about this great Pope before I began studying the Angels and their place in our lives.

Pope Pius XII

With extraordinary bravery and prophetic insight, Pope Pius XII warned his bishops that certain errors threatened to topple the very foundations of our Catholic doctrine. He came out strongly against those theologians who were questioning *"the angels are personal beings."*

During the Holy Year 1950, Pope Pius XII denounced this error in his *Humanae Generis*. So many of us, living during the time of Pope Pius XII, had no idea that theologians were already being used to destroy our Church. Today, many of us nostalgically long for the *good old days*. But, as Archbishop Fulton J. Sheen so often said, errors had begun to permeate the Church and the priesthood, long before John XXIII opened the Second Vatican Council.

Possibly the least known for his bravery and love for all mankind, *Pope Pius XII* was maligned and persecuted, and all because of his humility and modesty. The world does not know the bravery of this Pope. Right under the noses of the Nazis, he had an underground escape route, which saved the lives of thousands of Jews. He sold treasures from the Vatican to pay ransoms for Jews about to be killed in the Concentration Camps. And what gave him the strength and the courage? Maybe I should say *who* gave him the fortitude to resist the tyranny and the threats, to go beyond his role as Vicar of Christ to Catholics and become, as his Savior before him, brother of the whole world?

Although Pope Pius XII did not expound on his own devotion to his Guardian Angel, like his predecessor Pope Pius XI and his successor Pope John the XXIII, he did encourage the faithful, during a general audience on

October the 3rd, 1958, to "have a certain familiarity with the Guardian Angels."

Pope John XXIII

When Pope John XXIII opened wide the windows and let the Holy Spirit in, the Body of Christ discovered they, not the buildings, were the Church. Being told they were the Church, they realized they had a responsibility to know what was going on; they became involved. But, with that gift came the knowledge of the errors that were spreading, threatening to separate and, with that division, destroy the Church. We all thought it was new. No, it had begun; we just had not known it. I believe, the Holy Spirit sent His Army of Angels to possibly Pope John XXIII's Guardian Angel and said tell the Church so they can do something about it.

Pope Paul VI

With the advent of each technological age, man has become more and more dependent on what he can see and hear, accepting only that which Science teaches him. And yet, as in the case of water, can we see it when it evaporates into the air? No, we accept it because Science tells us it is so. Even though much of that which we accept as a fact, is eventually disproved by another scientist. But with this philosophy came the inherent danger of making gods out of God's creation.

And so, tenets of the Faith have become questioned, and very often the faithful do not know what to believe. Especially when even men from the Church espouse their own scientific, worldly opinions, and pass them off as doctrine. The shadows of doubt and disbelief, inspired by that dark angel of pride, have clouded the crystal truth passed on to us, throughout our 2000 year walk of Faith.

Pope Pius XII, in a radio message delivered in 1953, spoke out against this "technological spirit" which permeated the modern philosophy of his day.

Pope Paul VI also came out against our modern life-style which so romanticized the concept of depending more and more on how we look, what we think, our passions and their fulfillment, satisfaction of our desires, and personal gratification. We are so absorbed with things and thing doing, we have no time for the Word of God, and to assuage our consciences, we question the very tenets of our Faith, refusing to believe, simply mouthing words on Sunday, as we repeat the Apostles Creed.

This spirit of questioning which has been growing to such as extent that it has deteriorated into questioning and debating *doctrinal* truths such as: original sin, miracles, Jesus' words ("*Someone put these words into His Mouth to teach the people of that day*"), the perpetual Virginity of Mary, the Resurrection of Christ, and among many others, the existence of Holy Angels and that of Lucifer and his fallen angels. They take the encyclicals of our Popes and call them opinions, saying they have a right to teach their opinions, even though they are in disobedience of the Pope and the teachings of the Magisterium.

Pope John XXIII as well as Pope John Paul I, insisted that Angels had influence on politics and government. **Pope John Paul I** said,

"The Angels are the great strangers in this time of idolatry of the universe. Some Christians question whether in fact Angels are personal beings at all; often they omit all mention of them. It would be timely, therefore, to speak more often about the Angels as ministers of Providence in the government of the world and of men; in order to lead the faithful to develop an intimate relationship with them, as all the Saints have done, from St. Augustine to Newman."

Pope John Paul II

Pope John Paul II, aware of the theologians who have taken it upon themselves to dissent and to pass on their dissent to the faithful as authentic teaching of the Catholic Church, convened an extraordinary Synod of Bishops in 1985 with a view to establish a universal *Catholic catechism.* Shortly after, in his weekly audiences, he began to cover central tenets and truths of the Roman Catholic Church. He not only covered Creation, Original Sin, Redemption, the Incarnation, the Church as the Person of Christ, Revelation (Scripture and Tradition), the Sacraments, Grace and Morality, *he covered the Angels*!

Our Pope taught: "*The Angels who did not oppose the Truth have a two-fold mission: 'The Old Testament emphasizes especially the special participation of the Angels in the celebration of the glory which the Creator receives...on the part of the created world.' In other words, the Angels praise God in the heavenly liturgy, carried out in the name of all the universe, with which the earthly liturgy of the Church is incessantly joined.*"

He affirmed what the other great teachers of our Church have passed on: "*The Angels also take part, in a way proper to themselves, in God's government of creation, as the 'mighty ones who do His word,' in that they do God's will in the world.*"

Our Pope, along with other Popes before him, teaches that when we say the Nicene Creed, we proclaim our belief in the Angels. We proclaim, "*We believe in one God, the Father, the Almighty, Maker of Heaven and earth, of all that is seen and unseen.*" When we make this profession of Faith, we say we believe in Angels, in that Angels are expressed as the *unseen.* And so, when any member of our Church professes these truths and teaches otherwise he is not speaking the truth, whether it is that he is Catholic, or that he is loyal to the Church's teachings, or that he is faithful to the Creed we are all pledged to live. If he does not believe in, and teach the truths we profess in the Creed, he is not Catholic, and is highly answerable because he may lead God's children astray by alleging he is.

When we profess our Belief in the Nicene Creed, we pledge loyalty to *all* the Church's teachings, not to only those we agree with or understand, or can intellectually accept. It was at a time when heresy was again cropping up within the Church that Pope Saint Pius X required all priests to make an oath of loyalty to the Church. In *our* serious times, when most are confused as to what to believe, listen to our Holy Father and to your profession of Faith, at each Holy Mass, as you say: "*I believe in God....*"

From the very beginning of the Church, from the first Pope to our present day Pope, the Popes have acknowledged the existence of the Angels and have encouraged devotion to them. Believing they are inspired by the Holy Spirit, the Founder of our Holy Church, that's good enough for me. How about you?

***Bob and Penny Lord and Luz Elena Sandoval
at audience with
Pope John Paul II***

***"The Angel said to them:
'You have nothing to fear!
I come to proclaim good news to you -
tidings of great joy
to be shared by the whole people.'"
Luke 2:10***

Bibliography

Alexandra, Mother - *The Holy Angels*,
    St. Bede's Publications MA 1981
Broderick, Robert, - *The Catholic Encyclopedia*
    Thomas A. Nelson, New York 1976
Butler, Thurston & Atwater - *Lives of the Saints*
    Complete edition in 4 volumes Christian Classics
    Westminster, Maryland, 1980
Danielou Jean, S.J. - *The Angels and their Mission*
    Christian Classics - Baltimore MD 1957
Glenn, Msgr Paul - *A Tour of the Summa*
    B. Herder Book Co. 1960
Hogan, Richard & LeVoir John, *Faith for Today*
    Doubleday, New York 1988
Huber, Georges - *My Angel will go before you*
    Christian Classics - Baltimore MD 1983
Long, Valentine OFM - *The Angels in Religion and Art*,
    Franciscan Herald Press Chicago ILL 1970
Kelly, J.N.D - *Oxford Dictionary of Popes*
    Oxford University Press, Oxford, NY 1986
Lord, Bob and Penny,
    This Is My Body, This Is My Blood 1986
    The Many Faces of Mary 1987
    Saints and Other Powerful Women in the Church 1989
    Saints and Other Powerful Men in the Church 1990
    Journeys of Faith, Slidell, LA
Parente, Alessio - *Send Me Your Guardian Angel*
    Voice of Padre Pio - San Giovanni Rotondo, Italy 1986
Parente, Pascal Fr. - *Beyond Space*, Society of St. Paul 1961
Reilly, Robert - *Irish Saints,* Farrar, Strauss Co. NY 1964
Sheen, Fulton J. - *The World's First Love* - McGraw Hill 1952
The Precious Blood and the Angels,
    Marian Publications South Bend, IN 1977
The New Catholic Study Bible - Catholic Bible Press 1985

Journeys of Faith

To Order: 1-800-633-2484 - 1-504-863-2546 -

Books

Bob and Penny Lord are authors of best sellers:
This Is My Body, This Is My Blood;
Miracles of the Eucharist $8.95 Paperback only
The Many Faces Of Mary, A Love Story $8.95 Paperback $12.95 Hardcover
We Came Back To Jesus $8.95 Paperback $12.95 Hardcover
Saints and Other Powerful Women in the Church $12.95 Paperback only
Saints and Other Powerful Men in the Church $14.95 Paperback only
Heavenly Army of Angels $12.95 Paperback only

Please add $3.00 S&H for first book: $1.00 each add'l book - Louisiana. Res. add 8.25% Tax

Videos and On-site Documentaries

Bob and Penny 's Video Series based on their books:
A 6 part series on the Miracles of the Eucharist filmed at EWTN
A 9 Part Eucharistic Retreat series with Father Harold Cohen
A 10 part series on Saints and Other Powerful Women in the Church
A 12 part series on Saints and Other Powerful Men in the Church

On-site Documentaries based on Miracles of the Eucharist, Mother Mary's Apparitions, Saints and other Powerful Men and Women in the Church, and the Heavenly Army of Angels.

Pilgrimages

Bob and Penny Lord's ministry take out Pilgrimages to the Shrines of Europe, the Holy Land, and the Shrines of Mexico every year. Come and join them on one of these special Retreat Pilgrimages. Call for more information, and ask for the latest pilgrimage brochure.

Lecture Series

Bob and Penny travel to all parts of the world to spread the Good News. They speak on what they have written about in their books; the Body of Christ, through the Miracles of the Eucharist, the Mother of Christ, through her apparitions, and the Church of Christ, through the lives of the Saints both men and women and what they are saying to us today. If you would like to have them come to your area, call and ask for information on a lecture series in your area.

Good Newsletter

We are publishers of the Good Newsletter, which is published four times a year. This newsletter will provide timely articles on our Faith, plus keep you informed with the activities of our community. Call 1-800-633-2484 for subscription information.